The

Wielding

The

Wielding

J. E. Diaz

SHIRES PRESS
P.O. Box 2200
Manchester Center, VT 05255
www.northshire.com

The Wielding

ISBN Number: 978-1-60571-534-6

Building Community, One Book at a Time
A family-owned, independent bookstore in
Manchester Ctr., VT, since 1976 and Saratoga Springs, NY since 2013.
We are committed to excellence in bookselling.
The Northshire Bookstore's mission is to serve as a resource for
information, ideas, and entertainment while honoring the needs of
customers, staff, and community.

Printed in the United States of America

To Suzie

Source of Inspiration
Trusted Sounding Board
Venerable Grounding Rod

Thank You.
Again.

Acknowledgments

In addition to Suzie mentioned above—who put up with my incessant yammering about characters and storylines—there are a number of other people who have, in some way contributed to the completion of this book.

My thanks to Nat Dolsky, who has passed on but will always be remembered for his guiding light, Joni B. Cole, writing friend and encourager to keep going, Kristianna Lea, for an early setting-straight of what might and might not work, my real-life son Dan, for continuing to share the sort of outdoor experiences that inspired a chapter scene and character, Mike Scholz, for introducing me to the word, "oblibriated," Eric Roberts, George Kramer, and Barbara Palmer, for encouragement by asking how "the book" was coming whenever we visited, the folks at Translated.com, for their help with Saint Lucian Creole, Debbi Wraga, at Shires Press for her patience with me, again, and finally, a special thank you to Deborah Heimann, for patiently pushing me to reach into my head and pull out what I'm trying to say. Her guidance has been invaluable to this project.

Preface

Publishing *Wandering Spring, Notes from the Woods of Winhall Vermont* in 2016, followed by *Wisdom of the Vernal Woods* in 2017, it seemed reasonable to assume on that naïve first day of this project—while wandering into the woods for field notes in the fall of 2017—that 2018 would see another, similar volume. But what I expected would be a single season endeavor in the forests of Winhall, took two years and several border crossings to draft. It's been an enlightening journey; one I'm impelled to share.

Contents

Part Three

A Changing Reality

Part Four

No Turning Back

Preamble

Who writes our stories? Who chronicles the great and small events in our history? What details are overlooked, omitted, or even unknown? For that matter, what inaccuracies are inserted, asserted, or otherwise thrust upon generation after generation? But none of these matters. Even if every moment, every tick of the clock was chronicled with absolute truth and accuracy, the past, erased by the present, would repeat in the future. It's who we are. All of us. Human.

But what if we could evolve beyond our *sapiens*-centric shortsightedness? What if we knew the pendulum of history was swinging in our favor for the very last time? Would we change?

Ok, an easier question: Have you ever been faced with the shattering reality that what you thought you knew was only a part of the truth, or had no truth to it whatsoever?

Part One

An Emerging Reality

Coal-black clouds in an ashen sky dawned the last day of summer in Winhall, Vermont, with the absence of late-season bird song whispering the normal arrival of autumn. But what is, or I should say *was* normal, would forever change by that afternoon.

Chapter 1

Watcher Wandering Alone

September 22, 2017
Autumnal Equinox
Waxing Crescent Moon

Rested and refreshed after a lazy-day lunch, I wander deep into an unfamiliar wood, where vacuum silence descends on the forest. Exhaling slowly, I listen for a bird, a bug, a wisp of wind. There *is* no sound, no movement, save for a little black feather floating zig-zag to the ground.

Above, on a large limb of an ages old hemlock sits a curious dark lump: two obsidian eyes, blinking; two legs, visible as the lump unfolds, standing erect; two arms, one relaxed along its side, the other waving.

What is that?

Resembling a bob-tailed house cat, it climbs gracefully down the trunk with little primate limbs and no sense of urgency to flee.

This feels wrong.

Jumping off the trunk a meter from the ground, landing on all fours, it stands erect again and turns toward me, its obsidian eyes locking with my hazel gazers.

Stay focused.

With no visible ears or nose, its black eyes and closed mouth seem disproportionately spaced on so small a head atop a thick-furred—or is that feathered—body.

"I'm Seesterfekt Purbits," it says in a calm voice indistinguishable of gender, sending shudders of surprise throughout my body as it walks closer, the full glory of its gleaming black plumage—or is that fur—glistening in the open forest sunbeams. "But you can call me Seesterfekt, Purbits, or Seest if that's easier," it declares, stopping in reaction to my shudders.

It talks?

"Yes, I do."

I didn't say anything.

"No, you didn't."

What is this?

"First it was 'What's that?' Now it's 'What's this?' I'm alive." It giggles, tiny white chicklets peeking through coal black lips.

Humor?

"Truth."

I don't believe this.

"I didn't think you would."

It's a dream. It must be. This can't be real.

"Why not?"

Staring blankly into those obsidian eyes, my mouth is agape.

"Ok then," it says, nodding its head. "We can work with that."

But what is it?

"Again with the 'What is it?' I'm not an *it*, whatever an *it* is. I'm Seesterfekt Purbits—a sentient being, your friend if you wish."

Fifty years I've wandered woods and never have I seen anything like this.

"We call ourselves 'Peepl.'"

"People? That's what we call *ourselves*," I say, finally articulating a thought.

"Ah, good, found your tongue I see," *whatever it is* says. "Yes, Peepl. You stole that name from us," it continues, shaking its head and crossing its arms. "You're *sapiens*, humans, hominids, primates. These distinctions you've made for yourselves. You're not real Peepl."

"What?" I snap, crossing *my* arms.

"No, you're not. We are. You use the term but it's incorrect. We are the only Peepl. As a matter of fact, we were here walking on two legs, as were the birds, while your ancestors were still pooping from trees," chides the little forest thing, bursting into gut-bending guffaws.

I'm having a psychotic episode.

"No, don't worry, you're fine," it says between hee-haws, looking up from its bent over position, one tiny hand on a knee, the other flapping in my direction.

"What specie—"

"We don't," it answers, before I can speak my thought.

"Don't what?" *You little bastard. Are you really reading my mind?*

"We don't consider ourselves a 'species'... or little bastards. We know only that we're ancient: the Peepl."

He is reading my mind. Wait, he? I don't even know—

"Your propensity to categorize into gender is understandable, but our evolutionary path through your Garden of Eden...," it giggles again, "had a few twists and turns you're unfamiliar with, and we certainly aren't bound by your social constructs."

I'm not sure what all that means but it's too much to think about now. "So you have no name for yourselves, no species name, and no distinction other than 'the Peepl'?" I ask, still believing this is a dream.

"Correct," it says, with a toothy smile eerily too big for its face. "But we do have individual names, and I'd appreciate you using mine from now on when speaking *to* me, *of* me, or formulating thoughts *about* me."

I nod in agreement.

"Ok, now," Seesterfekt says, "try and imagine something different than what you're accustomed to. We don't conduct scientific study the way humans do. We rely solely on observation, with one guiding principle: Everything changes. We don't even have a word for specie—"

"Wait," I say, this time interrupting him, it, *ugh!* "You're saying you have a different language than the one you're speaking now?"

"No, I wasn't saying that. Weren't you paying attention?"

"Yes, I did, I was, but."

"This language you speak is infantile," Seesterfekt says, giving me another big toothy grin and a teasing wink with one eye, doubling the other in size. "It lacks refinement. It's very limited in scope. All your languages are. *Sapiens* have been using the word 'Peepl' throughout history, but the sound is from an ancient dialect. It means, to use your limited English language, 'Watcher Wandering Alone.'"

Seesterfekt takes a deep breath and stares at the analog watch face clipped to my belt loop.

Glancing at the watch, I notice it's 16:02, the exact moment of this year's autumnal equinox. *Why isn't Seest moving or breathing?* "Is that hair, feather, or some sort of fur?" I ask, hoping to break whatever has Seest spellbound.

Seest finally exhales through a nose now visible as one large hole centered below the eyes, smooshing them closed. "Fur is an insulting lexical slur insinuating a difference between *Homo sapiens* hair and other animal hair. There's only hair and feathers. Well, scales too. And nails and claws, but these are tools, not coverings. It's all keratin. Just evolved differently."

"Wait, scales? Where are your scales?"

"No, we have no scales. We have something like hair structured as feathers with, what's the word for it?" Seest says, snapping tiny fingers. "Ah, yes, photovoltaic properties."

"Ok, stop," I say, trying to slow things down and summarize. "Your name is Seesterfekt Cucurbit."

"Do I look like a cucumber to you?"

"What?"

"Purbits, Seesterfekt Purbits."

"Yes, Seesterfekt Purbits. And there are other People."

"Peepl. It's a double long E drawn out, not like when you pronounce People with a quick long E sound."

"Ok, Peepl. And you have your own language."

"An ancient dialect."

"Yes, that. What does it sound like?"

"Peepl talking," Seest says, deadpan.

"Yes, thanks. Like?"

"Sifōtesuy Yiyōzexulakez Vōxihōzey... O's are always long and emphasized, the other vowels short."

"What?"

"I said my name is Seesterfekt Purbits."

"Right, well, so," I say, more interested in attempting my summary than deciphering gibberish, "you have photovoltaic feather hair."

"It's a current-generating hair-feather structure that also absorbs the full light spectrum. Sort of like photosynthesis, but not exactly. Any light—sunlight, moonlight, starlight, lightning, even bioluminescence—stimulates the photosynthetic-like process... Something wrong with your jaw?

"My jaw? No. Why?

"It's hanging open."

Shit.

"Are you paying attention?"

"No. YES! Of course I'm paying attention." *What was the last thing I wanted to...* "You have the ability to read minds."

"Ah, well, about the mind reading—"

Mind reading? How about mind numbing. My brain is reeling from all this photo-synthe-voltaic-hair-feathered twists and turns through the garden of social constructs...

"I'll wait," Seest says, looking at the sky.

"I'm sorry. This is a bit much."

"That would explain your crucifixion pose."

"My what?" *Ugh, it's true. Why am I standing like this?*

"We'll talk again," Seesterfekt says, vanishing with a big toothy grin.

Distant bird song, an approaching breeze, and the crisp cellophane sound of dragonfly wingbeats situate my aural sense. The vacuum silence is gone. And so is my perception of reality.

Wandering the forest where I met Seesterfekt Purbits, waiting sometimes for an entire day, my only visitors for nearly two months have been hypothermia and doubt. But today, there's something else to do in another area of forest.

Chapter 2

A Pre-Turtle Conversation

November 13, 2017
Waning Crescent Moon

Arriving at the trailhead late in the afternoon, I grab my fanny pack from the back seat, throw on a blaze orange camo vest, and enter the wind-whipped woods.

'It's not a big deer, maybe a hundred-eighty.' That's all he said.

Skirting an endless labyrinth of wooded swamps, I notice a familiar vacuum silence descending on the forest. There *is* no sound.

"I see you could use some help," that non-gendered voice says.

"Where are you?"

"In front of you."

Seesterfekt materializes on a sodden, moss-covered log, half submerged in the shallow edge of swamp.

"Where have you been? And how do you do that?"

"Where I've been is where you haven't," Seest says, toothy grinned. "And how I do that is by what you call negative refraction, where the electric and magnetic properties of light are distorted."

"So you never really disappeared."

"No, we're not magical," Seest says, upward nodding at a soundless, leaf-filled whirlwind spitting debris, urging us on. "It was just time to disengage."

"You've seen him?" I turn to watch the whirlwind silently pass behind us.

"Over there." Seesterfekt points south.

"Far?"

"Very."

Dragging a hundred and eighty pounds of deadweight deer through forested swamps is no stroll through the Garden of Eden. Which reminds me... "What did you mean about the Peepl's evolutionary path through the Garden of Eden taking a few twists and turns?"

"Ah, that," Seest says, winking that opposite-eye-bulging wink and grinning that eerily-too-large-of-a-grin, when suddenly, the vacuum silence abates and the full fury of this clear, cold, windy day returns.

The idea of Seesterfekt Purbits being a part of reality seems more credible within the construct outside of the vacuum silence. Hmm, my thoughts are swirling like the winds.

"The Peepl have no permanent gender," Seesterfekt says, stopping to wait for me on an exposed rock in the water, watching me trudge, slog and climb over deadfalls. "Gender is something that evolution overcame in us around the time prosimians began branching out."

The sucking sound of pulling my boot from the mud echoes across the swamp, resounding in my head. *Or is that my brain collapsing?*

"Prosimians. How long ago was that?"

"It was during what you call the mid-Eocene epoch, about forty million years ago, when monkeys and apes started evolving."

Fascinating...but what was my question.... ah! "What do you mean by 'overcame'?"

"Well there's no need for hormone-induced gender tendencies once procreation is complete. We don't raise young or have family structure like gender-oriented beings do. Overcoming all this was an advantageous evolutionary step."

That sounds a bit pompous.

"Does it?" Seesterfekt says, shrugging .

Oops. Forgot the mind reading thing.

"I lost my gender two ages ago during molt," Seest says, eager to explain. "On that day I lay with a female and we molted together. The molt is our only vulnerable time in life after emergence. It takes two Peepl to keep our sensory domains strong because of the energy it takes to molt and regrow our covering within a few hours. The drive to pair as molt approaches is strong. It's a matter of survival first and procreation second. With entities such as hominids it's different. Your drive to procreate equals your drive to survive because having offspring is, in your psyche, a way of surviving. And it *must* be this way because of your short life span."

"Whoa, hold on!" I say, stopping, pulling back the reins on this runaway-horse-of-a-discourse on Peepl-mating and other foreign topics. "Ages, molt, emergence, sensory domains?"

"Watch out!"

"Watch out?"

"Yes, that dry mud you're on is sloughing underneath. It's about to give way."

A snapping turtle, exposed by the shifting mud, lunges forward, biting at the air, barely missing my fingers as I fall to the ground. Scrambling to my feet, I keep a watchful eye as it hisses with its mouth wide open.

"It's huge."

"Yes, it is," Seesterfekt says. "That's why I tried to warn you. This one killed a fully grown beaver last summer. Came up from below the water and pulled it underneath."

I've never heard of such a thing.

"There's a lot you've never heard of, a lot you don't know. Like how you've just destroyed this turtle's winter refuge."

After I apologize to the turtle whose expression appears to rather have bitten me than listen to my useless apology, Seesterfekt starts walking again, resuming our pre-turtle conversation.

"Two ages ago I was Koodj: Koodj Purbits."

"And Koodj is the mating age?"

"Koodj is not past the age of gender, so you're correct that it's the age of procreation, but we don't mate, we molt. Before molt, we have different coverings, but after the DNA required to procreate is shed in our covering, we grow our black coat, the one you see here," Seest says, gesturing with hands, from head downward.

"So Seesterfekt is an age-related title?"

"It's actually two age-related distinctions, the first being Seest— past the age of gender, and the second, a suffix as you call it, *erfekt*—past the age of adulthood."

"It's confusing. You're beyond procreating *and* beyond adulthood?"

"Yes."

"You said you lost your gender *two* ages ago. There's an age between Seesterfekt and Koodj?"

"We call it *ergohd— not* past the age of adulthood. Before Seesterfekt is Seestergohd and before Seestergohd is Koodj."

"You said *coverings* and then *coat*," I say, changing the topic, besieged by a sudden interest in specific details. "But when we met two months ago you said *hair-feather*—"

Seesterfekt raises both hands.

"I'm using words you're familiar with, ones that you relate to. The Peepl have a unique variant of keratin with properties unknown in any other life here on Earth. Covering, coat, hair, feather, plumage: Call it what you like, except for fur, anything but fur. Remember I told you what the Peepl think of that word."

"Yes, I do," I answer quickly. "What was your first coat like, and your mate, or do you say molt? What was hers like?"

"We don't use either term, but to answer your questions, I was what you would describe as tortoise shell, and she, a soft mottled gray," Seesterfekt says, sighing.

Like cats.

"Like Peepl."

"Of course," I cede, watching treetops sway above, my myriad questions swirling within. "How long is an age?"

"They're all different," Seest says, with a keep-asking-glint in one eye.

Ok, I'll bite. "How many are there?"

"Seven, by our reckoning," Seest says, again with a glint.

I'm going for the jugular. "How long do the Peepl live?"

"Well, it depends, my friend," Seesterfekt says, one hand grasping the opposite wrist behind tiny torso swaying back and forth.

"On?"

Seest suddenly stops, locking obsidian to my hazel once again.

"Our normal life expectancy exceeds thirteen thousand years."

"Thirteen thousand?!" I utter in disbelief, watching Seesterfekt vanish. "Thirteen thousand?"

"Pops, you alright?" an urgent voice asks from behind.

"Huh?" Startled, I spin around to see my son standing several meters away.

"Yes, of course. Why?" I lie.

After scanning the area behind me, he shakes his head and turns, motioning me to follow.

Great.

Back in the forest a couple of days after the arduous drag, embracing the undressed humility of autumn woods soothes my embarrassment, and my soul. Thickly treed slopes, now unleaved, reveal subtle changes in topography, unseen just weeks ago. Cold, dry air cools me as I climb through open woods to ridgeline where a house-sized glacial erratic rests, an ageless sentinel keeping vigil. Dense grey clouds with wispy white fringes float high above surrounding mountains where pine lingers on saddles and ridges, spruce clings to steeps and summits, and leafless Beech and Maple line mellow slopes.

Chapter 3

On a Craggy Outcrop

November 15, 2017
Waning Crescent Moon

"Good Morning!" Seesterfekt Purbits greets me from above while I fill my tobacco pipe on a craggy outcrop below a stout white pine. "It's a good sign," Seesterfekt says, backing down the mast-sized tree as I light the pipe and note the absence of vacuum silence. "Your senses are adjusting," Seest says, jumping the last meter to the ground, walking toward me. "It doesn't happen with everyone."

"How are you, Old Purbits?" I ask, as Seest sits nearby in front of me.

"Old and getting older each lunation."

"You left me looking foolish the other day, you know that?"

"Yes, I know."

"He *wasn't* far away, was he?"

"Not really."

"So you lied."

"I didn't."

"Yes, you *did*," I say, laughing.

"Yes I did," Seesterfekt says with trademark toothy smile, breaking into laughter. "'Pops, you alright?'" Seest imitates precisely. "You should have seen your face when you turned around and saw him," Seest says, rolling on the ground, then suddenly stopping, sitting up and staring into my eyes. "Your son doesn't think of himself as being adopted you know. He's a very well-adjusted adult."

"I know that. And I don't know how *you* know that, but can all the Peepl reproduce sounds like you do? That was an impressive replication of his voice."

"Oh yes," Seest says, still sitting on the ground. "And much more. Ever hear a bird but never see it, or hear a bird song that doesn't sound quite right?"

"The Peepl?"

"Yes. How about the sound of stick-snap or leaves rustling?" Seesterfekt says, standing up. "Nuts or seeds falling from a tree, but no animals visible?"

"Come on."

"It's true. What about the sound of running water where there is no stream, or a rogue gust when there is no wind? Lithe and swift footsteps in the night? Singing frogs that mysteriously stop? Bubbles from a still pond.? A ripple you assume is a fish?"

"You're kidding."

"I'm not. Ever have an animal see you, yet look away from you and not run? What do you think they're looking at?"

"But why? What for?"

"For fun," Seest says, little head cocked back, arms outstretched, palms up.

"So all the Peepl enjoy humor this way?"

"Oh yes, every one of us. Life is too short not to laugh."

"How can you talk about life being short when you live to be thirteen thousand years old?"

"Actually, we can, and *do* live beyond that, but to answer your question, thirteen thousand or even double that is nothing. The rise and fall of ice ages takes hundreds of thousands to millions of years. What's thirteen thousand? Nothing."

"And my seventy to a hundred? What's that? Less than nothing."

"It's a distinct quality you *sapiens* have," Seesterfekt says, "often looking at what isn't instead of what is; seeing half the vessel that's empty rather than the whole vessel that's half full. You spend your lives yearning for fullness because you believe it's something *out there*, something attainable *when* or *after* instead of *now*. It's the vessel that has worth, not what's perceived as being in it. Filling your vessels is an illusion. All that ever remains is what you begin with."

Though Seesterfekt's words by themselves could be taken as chiding, I'm intrigued. I reflect on them while watching Seest preen head and neck much like a cat washing its face, but with small hands of six fingers each.

Why didn't I notice that before?

"If you look closely," Seest says—now holding arms outstretched, grasping at the air while rotating both hands at the wrist—you'll see that there are two opposable thumbs, two of what you commonly call index fingers and two identical fingers in the middle of my hand. They're great at articulating and for grabbing anything, anything at all. And we can hang indefinitely with these hands."

"Can we talk more about the Peepl?"

"Yes, of course." Seesterfekt nods.

"You mentioned emergence, sensory domains, and your age. You're thirteen thousand years old?"

"Almost. I've seen 168,335 lunations. I'll be thirteen thousand years old on your Friday the thirteenth of December, 2069, during the day moon. Just 665 lunations to go."

"Day moon?"

"You call it new moon. We call it day moon because it's out all day, though for *sapiens* it's impossible to see."

"So you were born on a new, I mean day moon?"

"Not exactly born, we call it emergence. Do you remember I explained the molt to you?"

"Yes, well, I remember you saying you lay with a female, molting together, shedding DNA with your covering."

"Correct," Seest says. "These DNA strands knit together, rooting in the ground, growing into what resembles a vegetative bulb or corm, which is akin to your womb. We call it bulbing or bulb. But unlike you in the womb, we become sentient as soon as bulbing occurs. The bulb grows in the ground for six lunations and we grow inside it. At emergence, in spring, we're fully independent at one hundred millimeters tall."

"Very small to be independent. What about predators?"

"You should take time to absorb everything I've told you so far to gain a deeper understanding of the Peepl," Seesterfekt says, then vanishes again.

. . .

As I descend the ridge, pipe clenched securely between my teeth, I ponder Seest's twist on the glass-half-full analogy.

And the whole molting thing is an incredible way to procreate.... One hundred millimeters tall at emergence and fully independent? But what about predators?

Understory hemlocks dance in the downstream breeze of roaring cascades. Tons of water rush over, under, and around time-worn boulders. Cold spray dampens my clothing and chills my face—a day spoiler this time of year.

Away from the splash and spray, an eddy pool of bubbles hugs the shoreline—the antithesis of tumult raging in the watercourse.

Grand columns of oak on the river's north dwarf slender white birch on the south, where deep green ferns soften jagged grey outcrops, rising sharply above the cascades. A massive boulder lies in the middle of the watercourse, its flat top thick with ferns, well above the seasonal rage of rising waters.

Upstream, a downfall across shaded torrents grows icy baleen plates with frozen globes at the bottoms of each, hovering at water level. As I gain elevation within the ravine, the descending sun line warms me.

Chapter 4

Into Clear View

November 25, 2017
Waxing Crescent Moon

Opposite a good pool to filter for drinking, an enormous yellow birch clings to boulders at the water's edge. As I fill my bottle, a reflective lump on one of its aerial roots suspended above the water catches my attention.

Seesterfekt?

Wearing a big toothy grin, Seesterfekt comes into clear view, crossing the roaring flume on slippery boulders and icy deadfalls.

"Your perception is improving," Seest says, arriving on the shore as I finish filling my bottle. "There was light reflecting off the water, slightly disrupting negative refraction, but you saw me. Now, your last question to me was something about predators, wasn't it?"

Hmm, we talked about DNA, molting… "Yes. Emergence, right, I was wondering how the Peepl one hundred millimeters tall manage the threat of predation, that is, assuming there is such a threat."

"Oh, there is." Seest nods.

As I descend into a cross-legged position on a perfectly placed rock, I conjure all manner of dangers to something one-hundred millimeters tall.

"Our sensory domains grow quickly upon emergence—out hundreds of meters," Seesterfekt begins.

"Sensory domain?"

"Yes, I know what you're thinking: science fiction, fantasy, translucent blue orbs, trolls growing out of bubbles blown by children." Seest giggles.

"I've never heard of that last one."

"No? Well, be patient, I'm sure someone will make a movie of it. Now, where was I? Ah, yes. At the onset of bulbing, when we become sentient, we wear a sensory domain enabling us to read dark energy. At bulbing it extends about one hundred meters."

"Wear? And what do you mean by dark energy and how does reading it keep predators away?"

"Wearing is what we call it because, like wearing a cloak, the sensory domain flows with our movements. It's never exactly 'this or that' large, and we're not always centered within it. And as for dark energy, you might call it 'life' when referring to it collectively. Individually, you might call it 'soul.' We refer to it as dark because it's never seen, only felt. By reading this dark energy, we can discern intent from individuals within our sensory domain. If there's any threat to our well-being, we can influence the outcome and protect ourselves."

"Influence the outcome?"

"Yes, well, within our sensory domain lies our domain of impelment."

"Impalement!?"

"Impelment," Seest laughs. "Very different word."

"So the two domains are different sizes?"

"Yes, the domain of impelment at bulbing is one hundred meters and never grows beyond that. And unlike our sensory domain, the domain of impelment is rigid. It doesn't flow like a cloak. But our sensory domains continue growing after emergence, which begins our first age, called Faabl. During this time our sensory domains can grow from hundreds of meters to hundreds of kilometers, depending on the individual. During Koodj, our second age, a sensory domain might reach five hundred, or even one thousand kilometers. Once attaining Seest, we're able to expand this throughout our lives, though not all the Peepl choose to."

"This is fantastic. But the domain of impelment, why doesn't it grow?"

"The domain of impelment is only for defense. The ability to influence behavior at that distance is enough. We can detect predators through our sensory domain as far out as it reaches and simply avoid them. But when a predator enters our domain of impelment we can 'impel' it to do something else."

"Impel a predator to do something other than prey?"

"Yes, but this is impossible for you to understand."

"Why?"

"Because humans are unaffected by the domain of impelment." Seest falls silent.

There's something heavy about this revelation.

"Many years ago," Seesterfekt begins, "too many to count lunations, a branch on your 'family tree' that your scientists call *Homo heidelbergensis* appeared. At that time, the Peepl were numerous; our numbers reflected our ability to sense and influence the world around us. But that changed. Early *heidelbergensis* were wild, unlike anything before them: sentient infants with no capacity to understand what they were experiencing, yet highly advanced in terms of technology. Fire and weapons were their power. It happened overnight. One day, humans lived and roamed in relative peace, the next day, anarchy among their ranks exploded, spreading throughout the world. In a geologic blink of an eye, an evolutionary anomaly slipped into the void of an undominated creation and has held sway ever since."

"What do you mean, ever since?" I ask, remembering that *Homo heidelbergensis* died out about two hundred millennia ago.

"*Homo sapiens* you call yourselves: wise man, thinking man," Seesterfekt barks. "A few fossils here and there and *sapiens* think they know what happened in the past. Renown-driven conjecture!" Seest bellows. "All your *Homo* species—*habilis, rudolfensis, erectus, heidelbergensis, neanderthalensis, floresiensis*, *sapiens*, and there are many others," Seest says, chortling. "Look around! Where do you think all the variations in face, body types, eye, skin, and hair color, not to mention susceptibility and resistance to disease comes from? One species?" Seest asks, laughing harder now. "They're all here, today, all mixed in, even remnants from the lower limbs on your 'family tree': *Paranthropus*, *Australopithecus*, and others you've discovered, not to mention those you never will, ground into oblivion by the last glacial maximum." Seesterfekt pauses. "Primates, particularly hominids, have been mixing for millions of years. You're a result of all that mixing. You all are. Silly children, always fighting like siblings. Is it any wonder?"

"But why did the numbers of the Peepl change? How did the timing of *Homo heidelbergensis* affect them? What happened?"

"As I mentioned, the domain of impelment doesn't affect humans. Not anymore. From the early days of transition almost nine million years ago, when the progenitor of chimpanzee's and humans—*Sahelanthropus tchadensis*—began walking on two legs, until the arrival of *heidelbergensis*, eight million years later, impelment *was* effective. The Peepl should have known something was different about your *heidelbergensis* when sensory domains were not always able to detect their intent. The Peepl weren't concerned at first, thinking they could use impelment to protect themselves. It took a while to realize what was happening and adapt to the new environment. In that time, many of the Peepl were killed by the new humans."

"Killed? Why?"

"They were killed because they were feared. Your *heidelbergensis'* mastery of fire, and technological advances in tool and weapon making were fueled by fear. This new group of humans feared everything they didn't understand. They perceived everything as a threat. Mastodons, woolly mammoths, woolly rhinoceroses, giant flat-faced bear, saber-toothed tigers, ancient horses, giant beavers...the list goes on and on. These are some of the largest known to you that survived despite periods of overlapping millennia in which they faced extinction from constant pressure by *heidelbergensis.* But there are others your science hasn't discovered. They were simply wiped out."

"I still don't understand why the Peepl were perceived as a threat."

"Your *heidelbergensis* feared everything. It was as though they were dropped here from some other world, ripped from the comfort of their mother's arms and thrown away, discarded, abandoned. They were wild. Something happened at that moment in time forever changing the course of history here. The first hint of religion began; offering sacrifices spread like cell phone use today. Everyone sacrificed something for fear of missing out on the favor of forces controlling everything. It was *heidelbergensis* that started the practice of sacrificing their own kind to appease forces keeping the world cold. They were obsessed with displays of power over each other to impress or appease their imaginary deities. And that continues to this day."

I'm speechless, numb.

The roar of cascading water and tree-swaying wind within the ravine returns, no longer a muffled background to Seesterfekt's post-*heidelbergensis* history.

Chapter 5

Not Something Easily Explained

November 25, 2017
Waxing Crescent Moon
continued...

"That's a hell of a damnation," I say, finally able to speak again.

"History, yes, can't rewrite that," Seest says. "But remember what I told you in our first meeting: Everything changes."

I have no idea what that's supposed to mean. How can something that already happened, change? Sipping water, then offering Seest the bottle, I realize I've never seen Seest drink. *Shit, what if there are some weird microbes I'm exposed to?*

Taking the bottle with arms outstretched, tipping it up and falling over backward, Seesterfekt rolls down the bank, stopping just shy of the river's edge.

"You ok?" I shout over the roaring water.

"Yes, fine," Seest says, climbing back up, soaking wet, handing me an empty bottle.

Great.

"Thought we could use a laugh," Seest says straight-faced, standing in front of me. "Oh, and yes, the microbes will kill you," Seest says, hands dangling overhead, stomping in circles, eyes bulging, nostril flared, that oversized mouth baring teeth in a comical growl.

"You look bizarre," I blurt, trying not to laugh.

Seesterfekt stops turning in circles and stares at me motionless with that ridiculous face and posture.

Exploding into laughter together, we exhaust ourselves in convulsive guffaws, abruptly stopping, then succumbing, then stopping, then succumbing...

As our laughter finally wanes to smiles, Seesterfekt puffs into an ovate shape, that beautiful black plumage rotating and counter-rotating in minute vibrations from top to bottom, creating a thick, fine mist, disappearing into the air, returning Seest to normal size.

"You dry now?"

"Completely."

"Do you actually drink? And eat?" I ask, never having seen Seesterfekt do either.

"Yes, sometimes." Seest smiles. "Everything we drink and eat is absorbed and assimilated until there's nothing left but a small grain of inert matter in what you would call a stomach. Here, watch." Seest violently retches, then stops. "And that's it, no urination, no defecation," Seest says, talking between clenched teeth holding what looks like a grain of dirt, then spitting out the grain, as one would a raspberry seed finally freed from between the teeth, hours after being discovered.

"OK then... Can we talk about the ages," I ask, "going back to—what was it you called the first age?"

"Faabl," Seesterfekt says, still grinning.

"Fable?"

"Not quite. It's a double long A sound; Faabl, not the single long A sound of your English word, fable."

"Faabl?"

"Perfect! Now, Faabl begins our life after emergence. And if you remember, we're fully independent at that time."

"Yes, I remember. Of course."

"Then as you know, there's Koodj, Seestergohd and Seesterfekt."

"Ok, that's four."

"Actually, that's five by our reckoning," Seest says. "Since ergohd and erfekt are dependent on Seest, we consider Seest an age unto itself."

"But it's not really anything without ergohd and erfekt."

"*Homo sapiens*: wise man, thinking man," Seest says, with a headshake.

"Ok, ok. But it doesn't make sense to me."

"Do I have your permission to continue?" Seesterfekt asks, twiddling all four opposable thumbs.

"Yes, please. Sorry."

"The age after Seesterfekt is Manthasif, the sixth age, which I'll enter when I reach 169,000 lunations. And while Manthasif is not past material existence, that could happen any time after."

"Wait, if your material existence can end any time after you reach Manthasif, that would only be six ages, not seven."

"Except for the fact," Seest says, "that the seventh age, Satcher—past material existence and disappearance—actually exists."

Now I'm completely lost. "Disappearance?" As in different from when you vanish on a regular basis?"

"Very. Satcher is a revered age, when we're no longer seen or heard from. It also means Embracer of the Unknown."

"So it's death."

"It's not something easily explained to beings whose lives are so entrenched in linear time," Seest says, preening head with hand.

Not easily explained and not easily understood. Steering the conversation toward something hopefully more comprehendible, "You've been using the word lunations instead of months. Can you tell me more about how the Peepl keep track of time during the year?"

Drawing a deep breath, Seesterfekt drinks in the landscape. Maybe it's my imagination but I get a sense of what Purbits feels when taking in such a view, not being separate from the landscape, but a part of it, always moving, changing, growing—living and dying all at the same time, as if there is no time, no line between being and not being.

"The Peepl calendar," Seest says, eyes now focused on me, "is synodic, using the thirteen lunations within the four positions of the solar year, starting on what you call the winter solstice, which currently occurs in your month of December."

"This sounds similar to Hebrew and Chinese calendars," I say, immediately realizing by Seest's pained face that I shouldn't have interrupted.

"Early Hebrew and Chinese calendars were based on ours and are still in use," Seesterfekt continues, with a headshake. "Of course, alterations to fit *Homo sapiens* obsession with time as it relates to hunting, fishing, agriculture, scientific, sociopolitical, and economic concerns, have been, and continue to be made. But both have their origins in the Peepl calendar."

"Are you kidding me?"

"No," Seest says, again wearing a pained face.

"Sorry. Please, continue."

"The Peepl calendar begins counting lunations with the first day, whole, or half-moon after—or sometimes on—first position of the solar year, and ends with the thirteenth occurrence of whatever moon that is. Then the count begins again with whichever of those moons comes after—or on—the current next first position," Seest says, nodding upward toward the ravine in the direction of the rising moon, hidden by the southern rim.

I look in that direction. *Wow, the wind is really whipping treetops into frenzy up there...*

"What phase is the moon today?" Seest asks.

"Waxing crescent," I say, returning my thoughts to the conversation.

"You call it waxing crescent moon, which right now is about forty percent of the full visibility of its diameter."

Midafternoon, the moon must be up by now. It's getting chilly...

"To us it's one day before trailing half-moon. Your 'waxing,' growing visually, is our 'trailing,' because the moon *trails* the sun through the sky. When the moon shrinks in size visually, waning, it's our 'leading,' because the moon *leads* the sun through the sky."

I'd like to understand.... "Hmm," I mumble, shaking my head. "All these years I've never seen it that way."

"No, you haven't."

"No, I haven't."

"Nor have you seen the Moon during what you call new moon. We call it day moon because that's when it's visible, during the day, very close to the sun from the perspective here on Earth. We see it, but your eyes are unable to."

...the seven by their reckoning–

"Hominids—children! Always such difficulty focusing on one thing at a time."

"I'm sorry Old Purbits, you're right. But I heard you and understand how the Peepl measure time through the year, and I'd like to know how you're able to see the day moon, but first—"

Seest nods, extending an arm, gesturing that I should attempt the summation of the ages swirling within my head.

"After molt, the DNA strands from each of the two individuals knit together and then root in the ground growing into a bulb. The moment bulbing begins, you become sentient, yes?"

"Go on." Seest nods again.

"Emergence occurs in six month—"

"Lunations," Seesterfekt says, "very important distinction over time."

"Sorry, yes, lunations, six lunations later, when a new...person?"

"Peepl," Seest says, "singular or plural, only Peepl."

"OK, a new Peepl emerges fully independent, functional, and proportionate, standing one hundred millimeters tall. This now begins Faabl, the first age."

"Continue..."

"Koodj—not past the age of gender, the second age, is when molting happens. Seest—past the age of gender, the third age, occurs simultaneously with the suffix *ergohd*—not past the age of adulthood, making that the fourth age by your reckoning. Seest—past the age of gender, continues after *ergohd*, again simultaneously with a suffix, *erfekt*—past the age of adulthood, making that the fifth age. Manthasif—not past material existence, is the sixth age. And Satcher—past material existence, is the seventh age."

"Good," Seest says, with invitation in those deep obsidian eyes.

But invitation where?

"A closer look," Seest says.

"At what?"

"History," Seesterfekt says, vanishing.

Stargazing on this cold, clear, last morning of autumn, twilight waits below the eastern horizon while Ursa Major dominates the sky overhead, the imaginary line from Merak to Dubhe of the Big Dipper momentarily smeared by an Ursid meteor, a descendent of comet 8P/Tuttle.

Chapter 6

First Position of the Solar Year

December 21, 2017
Winter Solstice
Waxing Crescent Moon

First Position of the Solar Year
Five Days before First Trailing Half Moon

"Notice the alignment?" Seesterfekt asks.

"The line through Dubhe from Merak to Polaris?"

"Yes."

"I do. It's not quite straight."

"It keeps moving," Seest says.

"The line or Polaris?"

"Both actually, but more specifically, the North Star."

"I'm sorry Old Purbits, I'm not following you."

"I was referring to the time of my emergence, thirteen thousand years ago, when the Earth's axis was opposite what it is now."

"You mean axial precession."

"Yes, well, that's what your science calls it. For us, it's just another swing of the pendulum in an infinite effort to attain balance."

"Can you show me?"

"Sure," Seest says, bending at the hip with primate sway, little arms dangling, swinging back and forth.

"What's that?" I ask, laughing.

"I'm seeking balance." Seest giggles.

"Very funny, I meant the North Star at your emergence."

"Ah, yes, the Little Puller. It's right over there," Seesterfekt says, pointing into the sky. "The dim double star near Vega, about five degrees to the right and eight degrees up. The one that's about three hundred sixty of your light-years away."

I don't see it.

"It's about mid-shin of your constellation Hercules' leading leg," Seest says, still pointing.

"Wait-wait-wait. What did you say? How do you know it's a double star?"

"That's easy." Seest shrugs. "I can see it. It's known to your astronomers as f Her - 90 Her - HIP 87563 A – SAO 47037 – HD 163217 – HR 6677 – WDS J17533+4000."

Frenetically scribbling by the red glow of my headlamp while Seesterfekt continues staring at the heavens, I suppress my question for the sake of accuracy and take the time to enter the last numbers. "But how can you see that something is three hundred sixty light-years away?"

"How I can is far less important than why I can. This is a key component missing in human understanding. But that's a topic for another time."

I can only imagine...

"The Little Puller was the North Star at the time I emerged. It was called that because it appeared to pull the Circler around it. You know the Circler as Vega, which according to your mathematics applied to axial precession should have been the North Star. Polaris also circles like this, but there's no star within that circle from the perspective here on Earth. But close observation and agreeable consensus back then named the Little Puller as the North Star because it was more accurate as a navigational aid. It stayed closer to north than the Circler, which seemed to orbit it from the perspective on Earth."

What it must have been like listening to the knowledge of the Peepl.... Understanding so long ago, the concept of one celestial body orbiting another.

"It wasn't just the Peepl with this knowledge, it was your ancestors also. They understood stars, planets, orbits, the moon, even things like comets and asteroids. Yes, they understood these very well." Seest swallows hard. "There was no light pollution. It was easy for anyone to see the Little Puller. Even the light of a one-day-before leading half-moon the night I emerged didn't obscure it, though that wasn't the true night of my emergence."

This is a little confusing.

"The glacier fragment was enormous," Seesterfekt says. "It took about six lunations after emergence for me to reach the top. But that early morning, before twilight, I made it. Standing on the ice in the light of the moon for the first time was a powerful new sensation. I'd been absorbing whatever light was available through crevasses, refracted through translucent ice, and reflected in and under the glacier. But this was very different. Basking in potent-white light, there I was: a survivor from the time before the last ice age."

"WHAT?!" *I have no frame of reference for this...* "Can bulbs last that long beneath the ice?"

"Few of us made it through that time, but it's not what you think. Your science is advancing and your knowledge is growing. Some of your theories and hypotheses about the past are good, but the Peepl know things you'll never discover. My 'parents,' as you might refer to them, or Koodjdook—the sound from our ancient dialect to describe a molting pair producing offspring—didn't live before the last ice age *you're* thinking of that began over two million years ago. Though the Peepl have been around for many tens of millions of years."

"WHAT?"

"Didn't you say that a moment ago?"

"What?

"Yes, that."

"What, what did I say?"

"Yes, I thought so," Seesterfekt says, smiling.

Ugh, I'll just stop speaking.

"You should stop speaking more often," Seest says, leaning forward. "This time frame wouldn't have surprised you if you were paying attention during our earlier conversations, specifically on our first meeting, when I told you the Peepl were here walking on two legs while your ancestors were still pooping from trees." Seest giggles, slapping one knee, bursting into gut-bending guffaws.

Now that, I remember.

"And what about our second meeting? When you were trying to locate your son in the swamps. Do you remember I told you that evolution overcame permanent gender in us around your mid-Eocene epoch, forty million years ago, when monkeys and apes started evolving?"

I remember pulling a foot out of the muck, thinking the sound was my brain collapsing.

"It should be no surprise then that the Peepl have been around since the time your science calls the Cretaceous-Tertiary Extinction, about sixty-five million years ago, should it?"

"No. I suppose not," I concede.

"Ok, just checking," Seest says, toothy grinned and winking.

If anyone else spoke to me that way, I'd be pissed. Why doesn't it bother me? Is it the non-aggressiveness or the instructive manner? I guess it's both. Though Old Purbits is awfully insistent at times.

"I have no need for aggression my friend," Seesterfekt says. "You perceive correctly. I have always *been* and will always *be*, insistently instructive.

"Now, where was I? Ah yes... My Koodjdook molted in autumn just before the last great, short ice age, which your science can't fully explain. There was an entire generation of bulbs waiting in the ground beyond the ice flow near what you refer to as the great North American Continental Glacier."

The Columbia Ice Field in Jasper, Alberta. That is a fascinating place.

"Yes, that looks similar to where I emerged from the ice."

First my thoughts, now my memories. What's next, my subconscious?

"It's not possible for me to access your memories unless you're thinking about them," Seesterfekt says. "You're recalling this memory as a reference. I'm simply reading that thought. But yes, anything you've recalled has been accessible."

Great. "I'm a little confused. You and a whole generation of bulbs were in the ground away from the glacier."

"Yes."

"But you spent half a year under and within a glacier?"

"In a rare celestial event, an asteroid and comet collided, raining down mountain-sized fragments on what is now northeastern North America and Greenland, shattering the continental glacier in that region, sending equally large chunks of ice beyond its terminal moraine—tens of kilometers in some cases. Debris was scattered even further—hundreds of kilometers. You can see this in several of what your geologists think are glacial erratics in New York City. Some of those rocks were thrown there from the impact."

This is inconceivable.

"An incalculable amount of water vaporized, causing a global rain storm lasting six lunations. Each day of the deluge was colder than the one before. Cloud cover thickened with smoke and ash. Ice age conditions, slowly subsiding prior to the event, rebounded in the northern hemisphere. It snowed black, then gray, cleaning the atmosphere of particulates for decades before turning white again. Snow fell continuously in the north for hundreds of years after. Finally, the atmosphere dried, thinning the cloud cover, quickly increasing the global temperature."

"How could anything survive such a cataclysm?" I ask, astounded at the natural history I've just heard.

"That?" Seest shrugs. "In the grand scheme of planetary history, that was a hiccup. But maybe you won't survive what's looming."

What's looming?

"When the atmosphere dried, quickly raising the global temperature, it brought an end to the last glacial maximum. But now we're hurtling toward glacial extinction by *sapiens'* burning remnants of ancient life for energy, damaging the atmosphere and the Earth, instead of harnessing sun, water, wind, and lightening."

"I've never heard it put quite that way. But lightening? Can that be done?" I push, having some idea of the difficulties of such an endeavor.

"*Sapiens:* wise man, knowing man," Seesterfekt says. "'Can that be done?' you ask. Yes. If it held the promise of huge profit, it could be done, it *would* be done. But your priorities are investor returns, not what's best for the planet over decades, centuries, or millennium. It's who you are."

That sounds hopeless.

"Everything changes," Seest says.

"So what happened to your generation of bulbs? How long do bulbs last in the ground? How long can bulbs stay dormant?"

"Dormant is imprecise because we continue to grow sensorially in bulb when emergence is delayed. But to answer your question, prior to this event, no one knew how long a bulb would last in the ground, or under what conditions. We knew fire was dangerous to bulbs; many were lost over the epochs to fires burning deep into the soil, but swift surface fires had little effect other than delaying emergence for a lunation or two. Throughout our history, there were times when snow and cold delayed emergence up to a decade, but nothing beyond that was ever heard of. And bulbs survived local and even regional flooding before, but with this event, any bulbs trapped under the relentless flood waters expired and washed away."

A wave of sadness washes over me. "How many?"

"One-hundred fifty-six."

I was expecting a much larger number.

"We reproduce at a far slower rate than any other entity here," Seesterfekt says. "It was almost all of us."

"You survived because you were trapped under the ice," I mutter, nodding, imagining the cataclysm following the impact.

"Yes, I was 'safely' buried under a fragment of continental glacier, where my emergence was delayed."

"For how long?"

"Five hundred years."

"WHAT?!"

"Is that your new favorite word?"

This time I'm ready.

"No, *what* is."

Laughing, Seesterfekt continues, though the words dissolve into muffledness as mild hypothermia sets my mind adrift.

In the east, strips of fuchsia cloud float just above the horizon in a pale blue sky. Within the span of several blinks, fuchsia yields to hot pink, cooling to pastel, then glowing gold and brightening to yellow—marking the place where the sun will rise.

In the west, gray-blue bids farewell to night, a distant summit peeks over the slate-gray ridgeline nearby, and beech trees pop, echoing through cold, deciduous woods. A lone hairy woodpecker undulates across the horizon.

"Are you bird watching or listening to what I'm saying?" Seesterfekt asks.

"I'm sorry," I say slowly, my mouth less than willing to form words as hypothermia advances, sending chills throughout my body.

"Get into that nylon cocoon you brought with you and close your eyes for a while. You can listen while you sleep."

"How?" I slip into my sleeping bag.

"You are children, you humans, always asking questions about things commonly known. Sleep," Seest insists, as a pixel of light bursts from the horizon, quickly growing to a molten gold half dome too bright to watch any longer.

Blinking, I roll onto my back.

. . .

"Although trapped within bulb, my sensory domain grew quickly—at first hundreds, then thousands of meters, and gradually hundreds of thousands of meters. The situation was dire. Most of the bulbs were destroyed by impacts or subsequent floods. Others, like myself, were buried under massive fragments of ice debris for hundreds of years while the small ice age raged above, connecting each fragment with fifty meters of snow, compacting to form new ice. It was a dark day, my friend. As far as I could sense, only twelve other Peepl of my generation had survived the way I did. They gradually escaped their icy confines and were going about their lives."

Didn't any of the Peepl try to help you?

"We were sensorially connected. That was enough."

That seems cold and uncaring.

"You feel the emotion of being abandoned and assume I felt it also. The Peepl don't emotionalize misfortune the way humans do. You should work on that. Humanity could have avoided the whole quagmire of belief in omnipotent deities if you didn't emotionalize misfortune."

It can't be that simple.

"It *is* that simple," Seesterfekt insists.

"Air drawn through the ice by a meltwater stream formed a pocket above my bulb, creating space enough for me to emerge out of the cold, wet ground. The light within that pocket, though dim, was enough to produce energy. Confined again, though now above ground, I had to wait for the glacier fragment to move. But that was the hope; it was moving now, something it hadn't done for hundreds of years since it fell from the sky.

"After two lunations within the glacier, another pocket opened up adjacent to the one I was in. More light diffused through translucent blue, green, and gray ice, all adding to the energy I was creating.

"Four lunations after emergence, the glacier turned obsidian blue, cracking violently. I took advantage of the newly cracking ice and began climbing out. My size, stunted at half of what I would have been had I emerged on time, was now an advantage.

"Day and night for two more lunations, finding the smallest cracks to squeeze through on my journey upward, I followed every possible opening I could find till, on a particularly sunny day, when the ice was crystal blue below me as I traversed a tall enough crack to stand upright in, the glacier, bending from the great pressure exerted on it squeezing between two monadnocks, closed my route with no escape. I was trapped. Again.

"After nightfall, I realized I was less than a meter from the surface, as tiny cracks, just big enough to see a star through, opened above me. The glacier groaned that night in a way it hadn't before, when with no warning, the floor gave way, plunging me fifty meters from the ceiling of a vast cave into an icy torrent, washing me out from under the ice, half a kilometer downstream. After reaching shore, I climbed up the wall of the glacier to the top, where, as I mentioned before, unimpeded light from a one-day-before leading half-moon struck me for the first time. It was wonderful."

. . .

My eyes open to clear skies with the sun overhead. Rolling left, I watch Seesterfekt take in a deep breath and stare at the analog watch face clipped to my sleeping bag zipper-pull. Turning it toward me, I notice it's 11:28, the exact moment of this year's winter solstice.

Why isn't Seest moving or breathing? Wait, this is what happened at the autumnal—

Seesterfekt finally exhales through that nose I've seen only twice before... One large hole centered below the eyes, smooshing them closed.

"You slept," Seest says.

"Yes, I did."

"But you heard me tell the story of my emergence and conversed through thought. Or did you dream it all?" Seest asks, grinning.

"I don't know," I say, rolling onto my back again, staring at the cerulean sky. "Some say that life itself is a dream."

"What do you say?"

"I'd hate to sleep through something as precious and fleeting as life. But how is it possible for me to hear you when I'm sleeping?"

"Your ears never stop hearing, this I know. But it's *your* brain, perhaps you should be asking yourself."

I'm intrigued at the probability of having heard everything in my sleep. "Where are your ears?" I ask, realizing I've never seen them.

"Right here," Seest says, fanning open head plumage as a bird would spread its wing to dry, revealing what looks like a tiny subwoofer, pivoting in multiple directions.

"I've never seen, I mean, what the..."

"Incredible yes? Unique too. You've never seen and you never will on any other life form here."

"Incredible, yes. But did you have something to do with me hearing in my sleep, or is there some untapped human capacity I'm unaware of?" I ask, rolling left again. "Wait, no, come on. Damnit. Do you always have to leave like that?"

Part Two

Deeper In

Late-winter sun beams irradiate the back of my neck. A gentle tail wind wafts a bouquet of warmed skin and winter wear past my nose. Ice-cold churning water, reminiscent of glacial melt, splatters on the riverbank snow. Snow... There's still plenty of it in the woods despite the welcome warmth of 70°F after weeks of bitter cold. I wonder what's in store for the latter part of winter.

Chapter 7

Independence Day

February 22, 2018
Waxing Crescent Moon

One Day before Third Trailing Half Moon

Throughout the forest, holes in the snowpack reveal seasonal streams, reliable brooks, and roaring cascades, all coursing their way toward the river. It's hard to know where to walk, even with snowshoes on. Any slight depression in the snowpack can break through to a hidden stream. The amount of water running through the woods is extraordinary—it's everywhere. From splash of rivulet stepping down, to the white-capped roaring river, water sings its ancient, soothing song.

Otters melt over and under logs, slink across the snow, then slide into the river.

A raven croaks above—

Wait... that's no raven.

Smiling, I look up to see the imposter sitting on a large limb of an age's old hemlock.

Hmm, this looks familiar. "I'm mad at you," I say, despite my smile.

"You don't look mad," Seesterfekt says, challenging me in a brief staring contest ending in quiet laughter.

"You vanished again. You always do that."

Seest climbs down the hemlock trunk, jumping off about a meter from the ground onto all fours, then stands and turns toward me.

"That's the best greeting you can offer after two lunations? How are you, my friend?"

"Maybe the best greeting *you* can offer is to tell me why vanishing is your preferred mode of leaving a conversation. But I'm very well. And you?"

"Superfluous."

"Superfluous?"

"Yes, we all are. Besides that, I'm well. But I said that to watch your expression change."

"What? Why?"

"It's fascinating. We the Peepl don't have that ability. Oh, we can wink, and smile," Seest says, donning a toothy grin and opposite-eye-bulging wink. "But show the range of emotion in our faces that humans do? Impossible."

We the Peepl?

"Oh, that. Sounds Constitutional doesn't it?" Seesterfekt giggles.

"Wait-wait-wait. Can we please get back to the question of why vanishing is your preferred mode of leaving a conversation?"

"Ok young fellow. Let's move away from the river."

Pointing and walking, Seest leads the way to a blowdown clearing where sun-soaked boulders beckon.

There's something else on Seesterfekt's mind.

"You see that?"

"See what?" I say, sitting down on a warm, flat rock, and looking around.

"Perceptive faculty *is* something humans are capable of cultivating," Seest says, sitting a couple of meters across from me, the full sun reflecting off Seesterfekt's glistening plumage onto the boulders with disco-ball effect.

"What are you talking about?"

"You're correct. There *is* something I want to say."

Oh boy.

"Happy Independence Day."

Huh? "That's it?"

"Yes. Today they celebrate their Independence Day, which is still not much of an independence because everyone there, well, almost everyone everywhere, is still more or less under the reign of another, which is how it is with you humans anyway, doesn't matter where you live, you're always—"

"Purbits, stop! What are you talking about? I thought you were going to explain why you vanish in the middle of our conversations?"

"No, never in the middle," Seesterfekt says, with a headshake and one index finger wagging.

I wish I could just get a simple answer...

Water running through the forest draws my attention again. The roar of river as bass line, the intricate melodies of trickle and stream, muffled rivulet beneath the snow... It's a symphony to sooth my senses, yielding me to Seesterfekt's lead.

Ok, I'm listening.

"Thank you," Seest says, nodding. "Thirty-nine years ago today, Independence was granted to the island home of Koodj Tsitsyoos."

"A Koodj?" *That's exciting.*

"Yes."

"What island?"

"Your name for it is Saint Lucia."

"In the Lesser Antilles?"

"That's what you call them, yes."

"There's a Koodj living on Saint Lucia in the Lesser Antilles. I'll be damned!"

"Yes, I want you to go there."

"Go there? Why?"

"Because young Koodj Tsitsyoos has something for you."

What would a Koodj I've never met, living in the Lesser Antilles, have for me?

"Think of it as a vacation. It's been a cold winter so far and there's lots of snow coming soon."

"How do you know that? And do you even know that, or are you just trying to bamboozle me into agreeing? I'm sure Koodj... what was the name?"

"Tsitsyoos."

"Yes, that. I'm sure Koodj Tsitsyoos can give whatever he has to give to someone else."

Seesterfekt walks toward me and hops up onto my knee, those obsidian portals to Seest's soul striking my core. "Will you go?"

No weight to Seest at all... "Yes," I say, unable to refuse such a penetrating gaze. "But how do I find this Koodj? And where exactly am I going? And when?"

"Young Tsitsyoos will find you." Seesterfekt hops down and walks toward the other side of the blowdown clearing. "Travel to the Valley of the Free Peepl. Climb the

Southern Pillar. You must be there the day of the fifth whole moon: April twenty-ninth by your reckoning. Climb the pillar in the afternoon. The rest will take care of itself," Seest says, then vanishes.

Ugh!

Listening to the roar of the river, the trickles and streams, a slab of snow dropping to the rivulet beneath it, I remember...

Chapter 8

Back to the Point

February 22, 2018
Waxing Crescent Moon

One Day before Third Trailing Half Moon
continued...

"Now that I've agreed to go to Saint Lucia, can we get back to the point of why you vanish in the middle of a conversation?"

"No, never in the middle," Seesterfekt says, reappearing several meters away, with a headshake, and one index finger wagging.

Sighing, I drop my head.

"Vanishing is our way of leaving each other's company. It's our custom," Seest says, walking closer. "We leave when we want. None of us ever takes offence. We'll see each other many times in the thousands of years we live, so we just pick up the conversation where we left off. Besides, you forget that we can communicate through our sensory domains if we wish. Humans are different. There's always this sense of urgency underlying everything humans do, always this need to 'wrap things up' before going on to the 'next thing.' It's all part of your obsession with linear existence."

Seest is thirteen thousand years old... I'd like to live thirteen thousand years...

I stare at the river. My nostrils flare.

OBSESSION?! WHAT THE FUCK?!

My eyebrows squinch. I'm huffing.

ROARING RIVER...

I look away and gaze into the forest where dormant trees stand silent in the still air.

Easy big fella... easy...

I laugh.

Hmm, Seest vanished again...

Mixed precipitation and gusty winds persisted for much of April. But today's calm wind and blue sky bring an end to winter's last bid.

Chapter 9

Evolutionary Departure

April 23 2018
Waxing Gibbous Moon

One Day past Fifth Trailing Half Moon

"Are you enjoying the new weather my friend?" a familiar voice says from the leafless canopy above a grand hallway of white and yellow birch.

I stop to look up.

"New?"

"Yes, it's always new, every day. Never know what's going to happen."

Never know what's going to happen... I learned that last year on the first day of autumn. Shaking and lowering my head, I start on my way again. "How are you today, Old Purbits?"

"Unremarkable," Seest says, dropping from the canopy, landing on all fours a few meters in front of me.

Stopping mid-stride with my mouth agape, I stare at Seest. "I'd say *that's* pretty remarkable. And what's this new habit you've developed, answering my greetings with single words like *superfluous* and *unremarkable*?"

Seesterfekt stands up, gives a toothy smile, then turns around and walks in the direction I'm headed. "These words of yours are so limited. They can never convey the whole of our thoughts and emotions. I'm well. And how are you my friend?"

"I've been well. Glad to see spring finally break through winter," I say, catching up to Seest. "You were right about the snows."

"Of course I was," Seest says, winking.

Throughout the forest, pockets of saturated ground erode the snowpack. It's a loose-fitting jigsaw puzzle where grouse, turkeys, and juncos forage for food in the wet duff.

Further on, a song sparrow sings its territorial bid near the outlet of a swamp.

"What have you been up to during these last two months, Purbits?" I ask while studying the sparrow. "And where do you go when it snows as much as it did in March? And what do you do with yourself all winter?"

"What I've been up to these last two lunations is the same answer to the question of what I do with myself all winter. I expand my sensory domain. And where I go to do that is under the snow, the more the better."

The song sparrow is quiet.

"You bird watching again?" Seest pokes.

"Nope, just aware."

"Have you ever considered trying on a sensory domain?" Seest laughs. "It would fit you well."

They probably don't have any my size... "You were under the snow all winter?"

"Yes. Well, except for our brief visits. Do you remember I told you that I spent half of my age of Faabl under ice?"

"Yes."

"During that time, besides learning to expand my sensory domain, I also developed a love for being there. In the way that humans remember a sense of security as infants nestled in the arms of their mother, for me, spending time under snow evokes a similar emotion instilled during my years under the ice."

"Do all the Peepl do this?"

"No, just me," Seest says, grinning. "I've taken an evolutionary departure from the other twelve survivors of my generation. I'm not sure if it's because I was the last one to emerge, or if it's simply because everything changes. While still beneath the glacier as Faabl, my sensory domain reached the outer limit of what only a Seesterfekt could formerly reach—fully circling the planet instead of just the hundreds of kilometers that's normal for the age of Faabl. And I felt it, my friend. I felt everything."

Without speaking, we continue downstream along the swamp's quiet yet voluminous outlet. The idea of a planet-circling sensory domain sounds fascinating, igniting wonder and curiosity in me. But the solemnity of 'feeling everything' seems a weight inconceivable. A few hundred meters further on, we arrive at a swamp full of conifer snags, clumps of dead grasses, and small woody plants.

What a great place for a noonin' fire... near the stream... yet dry, rocky, south facing...

"Where did you want to make your noonin' fire?" Seesterfekt says.

Right, I forget about the mind reading thing.

"Yes, this is a good place," Seest says, acknowledging my choice as I begin gathering materials.

In a few minutes I return with an armload of stick wood and a handful of tinder. Using a ferro rod, I spark fire to life in a wad of dry grass. Seest nods in approval, adding a few sticks to the flaming bundle.

"I didn't think you'd like fire, being an ice mamma's child."

"We enjoy fire," Seest says, smiling. "The warmth feels good. We like the cold too. Both are equally enjoyable."

While our fire grows, we watch tree swallows fly a courtship dance above the standing dead conifers.

"Can we talk about the fact that there were only thirteen of your generation left?"

"Yes, in time."

Our small noonin' fire crackles streamside, mocking the gurgles of passing water. High above, a raven glides by, then returns with a potential mate. Circling together in a tight spiral while trading leadership with a gentle game of tag, they swirl out of sight on rising thermals.

Looks like 'in time' doesn't mean anytime today.

"Looks like," Seest says.

"I have my tickets. Flying out in four days."

"Yes, I know. Thank you. Now, you have a question?"

Ugh, I hate that. "Yes, I do. Why'd you vanish so quickly at our last meeting?"

"Jealousy," Seesterfekt says, still watching for the ravens above.

"Huh?"

"You had a reflective thought about how old I am. That gave birth to jealousy. Watching the river in that emotional state sparked a moment of rage in you. You diffused it by juxtaposing the still air and dormant trees against the river, but it was there, ever so briefly: Rage."

I nod.

"I've sat with many humans over the years, even as Faabl, and I understand you very well. Vanishing removed me from the scene and helped you restore your balance. Juxtaposing was your idea, though subconscious, but it worked well."

"I'm not as dumb as I look."

"Good thing."

"Hey that's my gag, god damnit."

"Yes, and I like it," Seest says, our growing smiles turning to laughter.

Adding a stick to the fire, Seest sits back and draws a deep breath. "As Faabl, contact with humans is forbidden."

Why doesn't this revelation shock me?

"Faabl is our formative years with rock, water, and wind. I honored this tradition for five hundred years after escaping from the glacier. But my experience beneath it did more than give me time to expand my sensory domain and bond with my icy confines. It affected my approach toward humans—another part of the evolutionary departure I mentioned."

"Were there any consequences from contact with humans as Faabl?"

"Oh yes, my friend." Seest laughs. "Yes indeed."

Although anxious to hear about Seesterfekt Purbits'—actually, Faabl Purbits'—meetings with humans, I'm curious about the formative years with rock, water, and wind. I pack my tobacco pipe and light it, waiting for Seesterfekt to continue.

Chapter 10

How About Thirteen Minutes

April 23 2018
Waxing Gibbous Moon

One Day past Fifth Trailing Half Moon
continued...

"Everything depends on rock, water, and wind. They are elemental—the first forces to be reckoned with. Rock, water, and wind are in constant motion, using different amounts of the same energy to move. It's this energy that the Peepl form a relationship with. Humans have the capacity for this relationship, but none cultivate it. Are you following this?"

"Uh, kind of..."

"Volcanos, shifting continents, birthing islands, the Earth's and Moon's gravitational tug of war, asteroids and meteors depositing aliphatic compounds onto the surface... These are all what rock does, as well as erode, which is interrelated with water and wind. Rock is the foundation on which everything else is built. It requires the most energy to move. It is the most powerful thing the Earth does."

"I don't understand when you say rock is the most powerful thing the Earth does."

"No. You don't."

"Ok, never mind. Continue."

"Oceans and their currents and tides, rivers and lakes, clouds and storms, glaciers and icebergs, even comets releasing *their* aliphatic compounds into the atmosphere—these are all what water does, as well as evaporate, which is interrelated with wind. So much of what water does is interrelated with wind. It's second in the amount of energy needed to move it. It is the second most powerful thing the Earth does."

"Wait, Purbits. Aliphatic compounds? I didn't think the amount found in comets and meteors had much of an impact—no pun intended—and I didn't know that they're found on asteroids. Yet you've included them with the elemental forces."

"Are you trying to make a point?" Seest says.

"Yes. It seems out of place."

"Does it? Your science is only now discovering these things, but I tell you my friend, these aliphatic compounds or 'seeds' as you call them, germinate an infinite variety of biologic life, scattered throughout the Universe. The total mass of these seeds will soon be estimated by your science, and then, young fellow, you'll understand why the Peepl give them such importance within the context of the elemental forces. Now, may I finish?"

"Uh, yes, sorry. Please, continue."

"Breezes, gales, hurricanes, and tornados. Dry air, humid air, cold, frigid, warm, and hot air. Whether it's the result of seasonal or daily sun-angle change, ocean currents, global spin, or brought on by the heat of volcanos, lightening, or the shock wave of something large entering the atmosphere—not to mention your insane MAD weapons—wind is third in the amount of energy needed to move it. It is the third most powerful thing the Earth does."

"Mad weapons?"

"Yes," Seesterfekt says. "M-A-D. Mutually Assured Destruction. That's what they're for right?"

Shit...

"Well, don't focus on that. No human would ever be crazy enough to use them, would they?"

Shit.

"Stop shitting and think about everything else I just told you."

I don't understand wind being the third most powerful thing the Earth does any more than I understand water being the second most powerful thing the Earth does any more than I understand rock being the most powerful thing the Earth does. I take a breath. "I can't understand this intellectually. And having a relationship with these things the Earth does? Doesn't a relationship require give and take?"

"Intellect," Seest says. "Humans see intellect as the one advantage you have over all your close and distant kin. That adolescent self-centered view blinds you. We the Peepl hoped the knowledge you'd gained about this planet and its place in the Universe would have humbled and matured you. But still you behave like unruly children toward the planet and everything on it, including each other. Emotional give and take? I'm sorry my friend, with humans it's mostly take."

Pipe smoke settles in the windless air beneath my wide-brimmed hat.

"It's time for you to evolve and mature," Seest says, staring into the fire.

A gentle breeze clears the pipe smoke. I follow its lead.

"So. How does one develop such a relationship?"

Seesterfekt smiles. "It was a wonderful time, not only for me, but for this area we both call home," Seest says, opening arms wide, laughing. "Though it wasn't without its dangers. After a day in the glorious light of a blazing sun atop the glacier fragment that held me captive for five hundred years, I waited for the leading half-moon to reach transit the next morning before leaving. That day I began my relationship with rock, water, and wind, climbing up the lateral moraine on the west side of the valley, then sitting, facing east for one hundred sixty-nine lunations."

"That's thirteen years! You stayed in one place for thirteen years?"

"Well, the very best time to form a relationship with rock, water, and wind is the immediate post-glacial moment when that's all there is," Seest says, grinning.

"I've tried to imagine what that time period looked like right here where we are."

"I'll tell you young fellow, this place was still covered with ice when I sat long for the first time in the valley west of here."

"The first time?"

"Yes, I've sat long many times. Still do. Now stop interrupting and listen. You may learn something."

"Sorry."

"Don't be sorry. Be quiet," Seest says, gently winking. "There is life in this thing you call a planet. You determine what life is within the parameters of your own understanding. But only a live planet can do what this one does. It must be born before any biologic life can form. It's alive, sure as you and I. We are its sentient self, not apart *from* it, but a part *of* it. You *could* share in the full emotional relationship with it, but your propensity to control your immediate environment to gain a survivable advantage gets in the way. It's who you are."

Seesterfekt shrugs and adds another stick to the fire.

"As I said before, the high valleys like this one were still covered with ice. Water flowed from these in a continuous roar. It was thunderous in narrow gullies below hanging glaciers that sat high above the valley floor on the mountain behind me. The sound was inescapable, breathtaking. Day by day, the rocks changed, expanding and contracting as they heated in the sun, cooled in the winds, and froze deep during long winter nights. Tiny bits of rock and sand chipped away at them when the winds blew. They never complained. They were glad to be out from under the ice."

Rocks complaining?

"No, never," Seest says.

Of course...

"Everywhere you looked, there was nothing but rock. The very thing that everything else is built on, and is most often covered, was exposed. And it was beautiful. There are colors in rock that rival that of bio-beings. It's a pure moment in the age of rocks—the post-glacial moment—when still unblemished by the hordes of lichen that so quickly take hold on them. Did you ever think of lichens as an invading horde?"

"No. I would never have imagined."

"Of course not, but a relationship with rock will teach you that," Seest says, encouraging me.

"But what if you don't live to be thousands of years old? What if you don't have thirteen years to sit around on a rock? And what if you're susceptible to hypothermia and don't have a means to survive the way the Peepl do?"

"How about thirteen minutes? In any weather? Certainly you can spare that amount of time and survive it with proper clothing. Maybe you can double that or work your way up to thirteen times that, or even thirteen hours. The amount of time is less important than the reason you do it. *That* is the give of your give and take, my friend."

Rocks in the stream and on the banks around us suddenly fascinate me. It's all I can do to focus on Seesterfekt's words.

"There were many rivers and streams and waterfalls at that time, all flowing into one great river on the valley floor. During the sixth year of my first sit long, on the day of the seventh whole moon, a huge storm came from the south, as they always did then. But this one was twenty-six kilometers high, well beyond the present-day height of what you call the troposphere. It was the only time—well, the first of only two times—in those thirteen years that I had to move for my own safety."

"Lightening?"

"No. The Peepl have never been struck by lightning. It was hail, as big as that stone." Seest points to a basketball-sized rock along the streambank.

My mouth springs open. I catch the pipe before it lands in my lap.

"The downdraft from that storm made your Mount Washington wind record look like a sneeze. And it was over just as fast."

I can't imagine the damage such a storm would cause now.

"Yes, but at that time, there was only rock, which, in some cases broke and cracked here and there. Oh, and there was the one hanging glacier that fell to the valley floor. That was LOUD. But by the next day moon when the hail had melted, you could hardly tell anything had happened."

"Next day moon? That's two weeks. How much hail fell?"

"Four, maybe five meters, depending on where you stood in the valley."

My mouth springs open again.

"Something wrong with your jaw?"

I quickly close my mouth. *But where did you hide?*

"When you decide to sit long for whatever purpose, it's smart to anticipate changes in your environment. I chose a place with boulders and lots of spaces underneath to move around in. I waited there till the storm was over, then squeezed my way through the labyrinth of boulders to a steep area against the mountain. I wasn't surprised at what I saw when I crawled out of the rocks. But the most memorable thing about it was that a kilometer down the valley, not one hailstone had fallen.

"Other winds blew hard continuously for days, weeks, even lunations," Seesterfekt says. "Always more or less straight, with the strongest and longest periods coming from the north. Those were cold days, my friend."

"How strong?"

"F-4, 5, maybe 6," Seest says, laughing.

"What? Are you talking about the old Fujita Scale? It tops out at 5."

"Yes, but the winds at that time didn't know Mr. Fujita," Seest says, deadpan.

"But you experienced this? How were you not swept off your sit long place?"

"My chosen rock for that sit long had many huge boulders nearby, scattered around it, diffusing the strongest winds from any direction. Always remember, when you decide to sit long for whatever purpose, it's smart to anticipate changes in your environment."

Smiling, Seesterfekt grows quiet again. It's a good moment for me to gather more stick wood.

. . .

Returning with only a few dry sticks, I find Seesterfekt reclined against a rock near the fire. Those little feet with six tiny toes—two opposable, four straight, all showing tips of retracted claws—resemble cats' hind feet.

"Did you, uh?" I say, pointing at a stout piece of log that has appeared where I was sitting.

"Me?" Seest says. "No. It was there before. You just didn't see it."

Chapter 11

The Sound of Rain Dripping

April 23 2018
Waxing Gibbous Moon

One Day past Fifth Trailing Half Moon
continued...

I place two sticks on the fire and pull a bottle of Belgian ale from my pack. "It's been a good day so far, hasn't it?"

Seesterfekt's eyes shine Iridescent green, like a whitetail's at night.

I've never seen Seest's eyes do that before. "You drink alcohol?"

"Drink it?" Seest says, grinning. "Of course."

Why doesn't this surprise me?

Offering the freshly opened bottle to Seesterfekt, I remember what happened the last time I handed a bottle to Seest. "Don't drop it."

"Not this," Seest says, taking it with both arms extended. Seesterfekt's eyes turn obsidian again after a hearty swig. "Chimay Red is a favorite. Did you know it's the original of the Chimays?"

"No, I didn't." *A favorite huh?* "It's one of my favorites as well."

"Cheers to that," Seest says, taking another hearty swig and handing the bottle back.

"Purbits! You finished half a seventy-five-centiliter bottle in two swiggings."

"No I didn't."

"Yes you did."

"Yes I did. It's how the Peepl drink alcohol—quickly."

"For the buzz?"

"No. Alcohol burns our mouths, that's all. Once it gets past our mouths, the burning subsides. But we don't react to it the way humans do. We don't get buzzed, drunk, or oblibriated."

"Oblibriated? You mean obliterated?"

"No, I mean oblibriated."

I've never heard of being oblibriated, though I imagine it's—

"What was it you said when you came back from gathering wood?" Seesterfekt says.

"Uh, hmm... Right, I said it's been a good day so far, hasn't it."

"It has. A lot better day than the one I had at the end of my first sit long," Seest says, with a headshake.

Ok, I'll bite. "Why is that?"

"It was my first contact with humans."

Seesterfekt takes a deep breath. I relight the pipe and take a swig of Chimay. *God, that's good... well, story time... guess I'll sit against this log I 'just never saw' before.*

"After thirteen years, the boulders were speckled with beautiful lichens of yellow, green, blue-green, grey-green—many different shades."

"I thought you didn't like lichens?"

"Just because I liken lichens to an invading horde doesn't mean I dislike lichens," Seest says, giggling. "I rather like 'em!"

Straight-faced, I glare at Seest and shake my head.

"Well, no matter," Seest says, shrugging. "Seeds of grasses and other plants, germinated in sediment gathered in pockets of lichen and in small cracks and crevasses in the exposed rock. Some of those lived. Most withered and died. The continental glacier, having receded several kilometers to the north by the end of my sit long, dumped endless amounts of water south. There, the saturated ground was covered in moss and littered with grasses and sedges, hosting many insects and small mammals. This was just half a day's journey away. And that giant hail storm?" Seest pauses with a headshake. "It was a result of the subtropical and polar jet streams colliding. Before I emerged from the ground beneath the glacier fragment, both these rivers of wind had crept the furthest north they'd been for a thousand years."

"Wait. If you stayed in one spot, how did you know what was going on half a day's journey away? And how do you know what the weather was like so many years before you existed?"

"My sensory domain. Remember that sensory domains read dark energy from every living thing: animals, plants, the Earth. And besides this, the Peepl memory of natural history is collective and communal."

"I didn't realize."

"I know," Seesterfekt says, patient and parental, placing another stick on the fire as the sun dips below a tree-lined horizon, quickly cooling the air around us.

I get up from my comfortable log backrest to gather more wood from the nearby forest. "Didn't realize we'd be here this long. While it's still light—"

"We've got plenty." Seesterfekt motions with both hands for me to sit. "Birds appeared: small flocks of snow buntings looking for seeds and insects during the heat of the day, ravens surveying the developments from above, an extinct jay—similar to your Steller's jay—harvesting lemming hair for their nests. You going to sit?"

I point to the few sticks we have left for the fire. Seest motions again. I cede, shrugging, and return to my log.

"Arctic foxes wandered near, as would an occasional lone wolf. But it would be a while before any large prey animals took up residence there, so predators didn't stay long. No, they weren't a problem really, much."

Weren't a problem really, much... Not very convincing. "I thought you were going to talk about your first contact with humans?"

"You missed the segue," Seest says.

"Segue? When? Where?"

Seesterfekt smiles, then stares into my eyes.

Weren't a problem really, much... didn't stay long... predators... humans... first contact.

"Well done," Seest says. "On my last day of that sit long, two young male humans walked up the valley on the east side of the river, crossed it, then began walking west toward the high pass behind me. They traveled light and appeared to be exploring without a care or worry for their safety. And why should they worry? They were young, invincible." Seesterfekt smiles.

Dusty old museum displays and *The Flintstones* come to mind. "What did they look like?"

"It wasn't Fred and Barney," Seest says, laughing at my memories. "And they weren't the ignorant brutes from your museum displays, standing near a woolly mammoth with a spear in one hand and a rock in the other!" Seest rolls on the ground in hysterics.

Watching Seesterfekt convulse in the growing firelight as the forest darkens around us, I question my preconceptions of prehistoric humans. And perhaps the company they kept.

"These young males were completely aware of their surroundings," Seest says, recovered from the throws of laughter, sitting up and closer to the fire. "Stealthy and cunning, they were two meters tall, had rich rust-brown skin—sun-colored and healthy—and long raven-black hair, worn loose and flowing. Each had fine leggings made of caribou hide, and a long bow of red cedar, wrapped with sinew and strung with the back tendons of caribou. Finely decorated quivers of beaver skin held dozens of arrows each. Their feet were shod with woolly rhino hide, prized for its durability."

"Rhinos? Woolly rhinos lived here? I thought it was generally believed that they never crossed from Asia to the Americas."

"It is."

"And that's not true?"

"It is."

"So how did—"

"Trade," Seest says, shrugging. "Humans had been trading here for thousands of years before I emerged. Each geographic location had commodities to trade that were desirable to others who didn't have those commodities. It was no different then than it is now. And it's no different now than it was at the beginning of your cooperative history."

I take a swig of Chimay. Conjured scenes of the past, skewed by the present, race through my mind. *Was it a peaceful process? Did these humans fight over 'trade values'? Was honesty the rule? Or treachery?* I offer Seesterfekt the bottle again.

"No, thank you," Seest says, placing another stick on the fire. "These two young males each had their own ideas about the Peepl from stories and legends they'd heard through family and others. One of them wanted to meet such 'kin'; the other wanted no part of 'feathered creatures' that can vanish and reappear somewhere else. It was *that* one who spotted me sitting on the boulder and immediately drew his bow. The speed and grace with which he slid the bow off his back, pulled an arrow from the quiver, nocked it, and took aim at me was impressive."

"How far away were they?"

"About three-hundred meters."

"So there's no way you were in any danger."

"He loosed that arrow in an arc compensating for distance, wind force and direction, as well as temperature and humidity—"

"Wait-wait-wait. These are things modern-day snipers with extremely long-range rifles take into consideration."

"—And that arrow would have hit me if I didn't move."

"Why didn't you vanish when the two appeared?"

"Faabl can't vanish. Neither can Koodj. Pre-molt covering doesn't have the light-distorting negative refraction characteristics of a Seest."

Shit.

"Yes, I had a similar thought when that human nocked his arrow and started calculating its trajectory." Seesterfekt laughs.

"But you knew you couldn't vanish, so why not hide before they spotted you?"

"We're not without fault, especially when young. We experience similar inner conflicts as you when it comes to convention versus exploration, which is why contact with humans was forbidden as Faabl and Koodj since the time humans became unaffected by the domain of impelment."

I raise my eyebrows, catching what may have been a mistake for Seesterfekt to say, and something I haven't realized until now. "If Tsitsyoos is Koodj, how can he meet with me?"

"He who? Tsitsyoos? Koodj? Ah, that," Seest says, shrugging. "That's different. You'll see. It'll be fine."

Sounds like a brushing off—

"What happened that day was a good example of why The Forbidden exists. I thought humans would embrace the Peepl once they saw we weren't a threat. I thought I could convince them."

"So you defied the wisdom of convention and set off to prove yourself right," I say, taking some pride in the fact that we humans have at least something in common with the Peepl.

"Yes."

"So what happened?"

"Both humans ran toward me, with the one who shot leading, knocking another arrow on the run, yelling that it was their duty to protect their family band, and that 'those creatures' were dangerous. The non-aggressive one tried discouraging the pursuit, insisting that there was nothing to be afraid of. Running faster than his companion's calculated risk of shooting over his head, he was struck in the back with an arrow, knocking him off his feet, tumbling his body into a heap a few meters away."

"What did you do?"

"I suggested the raven watching us from above, bluff an attack on the aggressive one to distract him while I tried to heal his companion."

"Heal?" I say, squinching my eyebrows.

"It's rare. The Peepl traditionally don't interfere with incidents involving humans, but this was my fault. The whole thing happened because of my insistence that I was right."

"But wouldn't healing the human be violating convention again?"

Seest shrugs. "I was on a roll."

A coyote's lone howl from the darkened forest punctuates Seesterfekt's statement.

"The raven was killed on the wing," Seest says, gazing at the moon, now beyond transit. "At that point I jumped on the back of the injured human and began removing the arrow."

"The other one didn't shoot you?"

"No," Seest says, now eyeing Venus in the west, chasing sunset glow. "Not at that moment. He waited till I pulled the arrow out, then dropped to the ground attempting a shot from ten meters away."

"And?"

"Broke his right elbow and knee landing on a large, sharp rock firmly imbedded in the ground. His arrow never left the bow."

He must have been raging mad.

"You can't imagine the rage of this one. He was exceptionally good at hate—beaten by brothers and uncles as a child, ignored by his mother. He was angry and voracious in his appetite for revenge, exacting it on anyone, anytime. The male with him was his only friend, the only human who didn't abandon him because of his temper and mistreatment. And now, there he was—a heap lying on the ground... And I was to blame. But broken bones didn't stop humans in those days, and this one kept coming, crawling and spitting obscenities, entranced in his obsession to kill me. Quickly jumping off his friend, I backed away, slowly, as he crawled closer, never wavering from the countenance of hatred till he fell over dead, shot through the base of his skull with an arrow from behind."

"His friend shot him?"

"Yes," Seesterfekt says, solemnly. "But the injured human didn't kill his friend just to save me. He did it to end a life of perpetrating violence. His friend had killed once and left many more scarred and mangled from his cruelty. Attacking me without provocation was the spear that broke the mammoth's back, to use a very old phrase," Seest says, subduing a smile.

"This human who saved your life, what was his name?"

"Ptk. It means gratitude."

"Gratitude?"

"Yes. Ptk is the sound of rain dripping, rain dripping means plants will grow, plants growing means animals will come, animals coming means full stomachs, full stomachs bring contentment, and contentment brings gratitude. Very simple language."

"That's simple?"

"Yes, because you create a network of associative memory, input by rote, which is then quickly accessed."

I'm not so sure Seesterfekt is right about this one.

"In another example," Seest says, "sswhoo is the sound of snow and wind. The sound of snow and wind means winter. Making that sound while bending both arms at the elbows, waving toward yourself, means winter is coming soon. Winter coming soon means fewer animals, fewer animals mean less food, less food means empty stomachs, and empty stomachs bring discontent. Such a statement of fact would have been presented in a meeting of a larger family band to address the need to relocate."

Still not so sure Seest is right.

"The nuances of inflection and emphasis in gesture are what really made that language a beautiful expression of the human mind and body," Seesterfekt says. "It's a shame it died out."

"Why did it?"

"Increasing population, new ideas, new ways of speaking that were faster at getting a point across. But richness of content gave way to snippets of information, often leaving doubt as to the precise meaning of the words and intent of the speaker. This led to increased fighting among family bands and larger bands of many families. And eventually, the decline of long-distance trade."

Seesterfekt yields the moment to a nearby coyote choir, yipping beneath a post-transit moon. A faint stick-snap ends the chorus as I gather cooling embers, reigniting the fire with a lengthy blow. Taking a swig of ale and reclining against my log backrest, I wait for Seest to continue.

"Ptk looked at me with a stern, but grateful face, conveying acceptance in killing his friend to save me," Seest says, placing a stick on the newly stoked embers. "It was at that moment that I gained an appreciation for human facial expression. You convey so much with your eyes and faces. It's really quite unique."

"How badly was Ptk injured?"

"Ptk's wound wasn't deep or serious. The arrow chipped his shoulder blade and lodged between the fourth and fifth rib without penetrating his chest cavity. He healed quickly without infection, though the sensitivity in his ribs lingered till death."

"How old was he, and how long did he live?"

"Ptk was sixteen years when we met, and lived to be forty-five. He died of sepsis. It was the result of a cut from an unsterilized stone knife blade."

"Humans sterilized their knives back then?"

"Knives, spears, arrowheads, blade-stones, anything used to process meat for eating," Seesterfekt says, nodding. "Sterilizing was easy. Fire was readily available each day. Having rotten flesh stuck to your hunting and meat-processing tools was considered a sign of mental illness since it was widely known that sickness often followed such unclean practice."

"This is fascinating. I had no idea that human thought was so advanced over twelve thousand years ago."

"Advanced?" Seest laughs. "They were observant. They had to be. Their lives depended on it. Not like this present age, when so much of living is done for you. But I told you this story in part to illustrate why I defied the 'wisdom' of convention, as you put it. Some humans *can* be trusted."

"And some simply *cannot*."

Seesterfekt nods, looking east where barred owls call from a distant swamp, then stares at a moonlit ribbon of smoke rising from our fire pit. "Ptk had a mate and two daughters, all killed in a flood when he was twenty. After I helped Ptk with the ritual burning of his family's bodies, we began wandering together. Whenever he met humans willing to listen, he'd explain how the Peepl were harmless, even benevolent, and there was no reason to fear us. For twenty-five years Ptk told his stories and was welcomed wherever he went. He was well-known for his support of the Peepl, even though few humans had ever seen one of us."

Smiling, Seest pauses. We listen to the ancient dialects of owls and stream.

"One very cold day, while Ptk was washing in a small stream, one of the humans who didn't agree with Ptk's view of the Peepl sent his young daughter named Shri-ti upstream to find Ptk and mate with him. The idea was for several humans of Shri-ti's larger family band to catch Ptk with the young girl and discredit him."

"How young was this Shri-ti?"

"Much too young for mating," Seest says, with a headshake.

"And her father sent her?"

"Yes, I'm afraid so. I warned Ptk, who came out of the water and put his breech and leggings on before the girl arrived. But he didn't take my advice to leave."

"Another instance where you interfered with human interaction. Is this a habit of yours?"

"It has become so, I'm afraid."

"So what happened?"

"When young Shri-ti arrived, naked, shivering, and crying quietly, Ptk motioned for her to come out of the water. Bending on one knee as she approached, he wrapped her in skins and held her tight to warm her."

"And that's when her father and the others showed up?"

"Yes." Seest nods. "Ptk cradled Shri-ti in his arms, walked over to the small crowd, and handed Shri-ti to the father. He addressed each one of them, looking in their eyes as he spoke. Ptk explained that the father set a trap using Shri-ti to discredit him, and that it was me who warned him."

"You were there, out in the open, visible to the humans?"

"Yes, it would have been a good day for the Peepl had the situation unfolded differently."

"What happened?"

"The father would have been cast from the family band if it hadn't been for Ptk's tireless oration, insisting that the father was not bad, but did a bad thing. That night the father took Shri-ti with him to the fire of Ptk. It was customary to make an offering of gratitude to someone when they went to such lengths as Ptk did to be fair and forgiving of a wrong done to them. As reconciliation, the father offered Shri-ti to Ptk as a mate."

"What?"

"Yes. The thing here was that an offer made as reconciliation could not be refused. Doing so would insult the person making the offer and was considered a sign that whatever lengths the other person went to, they were insincere. It was the father's plan B to discredit Ptk."

"Are kidding me?"

"No, young fellow. I wish I was."

"So what happened?"

"The father stood in front of Ptk with Shri-ti between them when he made the offer of reconciliation. When Ptk refused without taking a moment to think about it, the father, in his rage, stabbed Shri-ti in the back, threw her to the ground and lunged at Ptk."

"What the F—"

"After a brief scuffle, Ptk took the knife away from the father, who ran away into the night. It was then that Ptk realized he'd been stabbed in the abdomen."

"So that's where Ptk got the infection from?"

"Yes."

"And Shri-ti?"

"Conscious till her moment came, as dignified as a child can be in such a circumstance, she bled to death in Ptk's arms."

My eyes fill with tears.

"Ptk held Shri-ti till her body turned cold, quietly rocking back and forth the way he used to with his own children, lost so many years earlier. As we did with them, Ptk and I prepared a fire and burned Shri-ti's body. He didn't clean his wound till after the fire cooled the next day. By then, infection had set in. He died well four days later, sitting up, calm and reserved, despite chills and discomfort."

"And the father?"

"He was stripped, bent backwards and tied to a large rock, then spat, urinated, and defecated on. This was done far enough away from the village where no one would hear him scream as his skin, tightened by dehydration and exposure, cracked open, exposing his unprotected flesh to infection, insects, and scavengers."

That's a decisive action... holy shit...

"It was customary in those days. A responsibility of the perpetrator's family band and a way of restoring trust in that band. Within this custom, members of the victim's immediate family, though forbidden to participate, also attended as witnesses to the restoration of the guilty's family honor."

"So who witnessed for Ptk's family? Didn't they die in a flood?"

"I did," Seesterfekt says. "Without a witness from each victim's family, the punishment couldn't be carried out."

"So who witnessed for Shri-ti?"

"I did."

"The humans accepted you? As a witness? For both?"

"Heinous crimes met with heinous punishments," Seesterfekt says. "Humans here at that time believed that once someone committed such offenses, they had reached a place of no return, and that it was in the best interest of all to cull these from the population. They weren't about to let what the father did go unpunished on a technicality.

"Their system worked for many thousands of years, but like all things human, it became corrupt and twisted over time—good ideas, abused by the few, wreaking havoc on the many.

"Ptk's friend's death and the murders of Ptk and Shri-ti were a consequence of early contact with humans. The Forbidden wasn't put in place just for the Peepl. It was put in place because it's wise to have three thousand years of observing humans before dealing with them. That hasn't changed. Just the number of the Peepl has. Greatly."

Yawning, I stand and stretch, stumbling over something where the stick-wood had been as I leave the light of our fire to pee among the darkened forest cover of spruce. Venus, setting through deciduous trees beyond the spruces, catches my attention as I relieve myself. When I return, the fire has a few more sticks on it.

Chapter 12
Restless

April 23 2018
Waxing Gibbous Moon

One Day past Fifth Trailing Half Moon
continued...

"I appreciate you telling me these stories," I say, sitting down.

"I appreciate you listening."

"So you've sat long many times?"

"Yes. I made a habit of sitting long as Faabl whenever a relationship with a human ended as a result of their death. That custom began with Ptk and ended with Ankit-ip, four hundred forty-six years later. The tundra had come and gone here. It was a remarkably fast transition, though there were still meadows with sedges, grasses, and alpine flowers dispersed among the forested mountains and valleys. Thickets of willow and alder grew, as they do now, along rivers, streams, lakes, and ponds. Black spruce, balsam fir, and tamarack grew in the lowlands. Red spruce grew thick in steep sections of valleys and mountains. There were aspen and thick woods of yellow birch. Ash and mountain ash mixed with and outgrew the conifers in open places. White pine grew here and there, with some trees already forty meters high. But hemlock was the dominant conifer in deep, broad valleys, with thick, tall stands of sixty meters or more. Summers were dry and hot, and winters were nearly snowless. But every year, a bitter cold snap killed less-hardy plants whose seeds made it this far north, carried on the winds or by seasonal migrators. The air was dry, but plenty of water still flowed from glaciers in the highest highlands, where the tundra creeped up shallow valleys. It was there that I met Ankit-ip."

"Does Ankit-ip mean something?"

"It does. It's the same language as Ptk's, though it had evolved over hundreds of years. It means 'restless.' Ankit-ip is the sound of a hiccup, hiccupping means you ate too fast, eating too fast means you have too much on your mind, too much on your mind makes you restless. It was also a playful nickname and often given to infants in the womb who moved around a lot. But Ankit-ip's mother kept that name for her child after birth. As I remember, it was the only time this playful nickname was given as a real name."

"So essentially, she named her kid hiccup."

"No, Ankit-ip was the *sound* of a hiccup, but that sound, when applied as a name meant 'restless.'"

"Right. Simple." I wink, reaching for more firewood from the well-stocked pile. "Weren't we just about out?" I say, glancing sideways at Old Purbits. "That stick-snap after the coyote choir began—before explaining how you gained an appreciation for human facial expression... Was that you?"

Seesterfekt looks off into the dark woods, whistling the fluty notes of a hermit thrush.

"That's impossible! How could you move so fast and silent?"

"It's the alcohol," Seest says. "And I wasn't silent. You heard the stick-snap. Though it wasn't really a stick, it was an imitation of stick-snap as a diversion so I could—"

"The alcohol? I thought you said alcohol didn't affect you. You collected this pile of sticks in the time it took the coyotes to sing and for me to rekindle the fire? Come on, that was a minute at most. You've got to be kidding."

"No, I'm not kidding. And I never said alcohol doesn't affect the Peepl. I said we don't react to it the way humans do. We drink it quick, it metabolizes quick, and we have to burn it off quick. Well, within a couple of hours or it becomes toxic. It's quite deadly."

Seesterfekt looks toward the moonless west. Preserving the visual peace of starlit woods, I place only one stick on our small fire, and move closer to benefit from its precious heat. A slow-moving satellite passes overhead. Seest eyes it, grunts, and looks away.

"How did you and Ankit-ip meet?"

"Humans have always had an insatiable thirst for exploring," Seesterfekt says, moving closer to the fire. "I knew that eventually one would come to the highlands, and I knew that one would be Ankit-ip. Always seeking solitude that one was, though I didn't expect to meet quite the way we did." Seest laughs. "Ankit-ip was running away from a large cat that also came to the highlands for solitude—to raise her kittens."

I'm getting tired... and thinking is easier than articulating... may I—

"Yes, go ahead," Seest says.

What do you mean by large cat?

"At that time, the 'prehistoric' big cats as you call them, were gone from this area. There were too many humans."

Humans were hunting them?

"Hunting big cats was more about driving them away than actually killing them, though it did happen occasionally. But the cats dwindled because of constant harassment and competition for resources."

So it was a catamount that chased Ankit-ip?

"Yes, what you call a mountain lion, puma, or catamount. A big one."

Please, continue.

"There was no place to hide and the cat was closing. Running toward the rock I was on, Ankit-ip drew the cat into my domain of impelment, where I suggested it return to her kittens a few hundred meters away. As Ankit-ip ran past me, the cat gave up the chase, one stride away from catching its quarry."

"What was Ankit-ip thinking as he ran past you?" I say, energized by the suspense.

"Ankit-ip was female," Seest says, with a headshake. "Your gender indoctrination runs deep."

I suppose it does. "Sorry. What was *she* thinking?"

"Resignation. Knowing it was unwise for women to leave the safety of the family encampment when menstruating, Ankit-ip had a habit of doing it anyway, and this time, she thought, was the end. It was the only reason the cat was chasing her. Ankit-ip was the stealthiest stalker in her band—quite an achievement for a seventeen-year-old—and would have snuck past the cat if it wasn't for the thick scent she carried with her."

"What did Ankit-ip look like?" Scenes from *The Flintstones* flash through my mind again.

"She was no Wilma or Betty, and she wasn't frail or frightened looking like those ridiculous museum manikins either," Seesterfekt says, laughing. "Ankit-ip was just under two meters tall, completely aware of her surroundings, cunning, and stealthy. She wore breechclout, leggings, and a shirt made of fine calf hide from a now extinct animal your science calls stag-moose. It fit loose and untucked, allowing free movement of her arms and torso, and was decorated with carved bone ornaments secured with sinew, not hanging, like so many other females of her day preferred. She had long, flat-black hair—a rarity, and cryptic advantage. And her skin was a rich rust-brown like Ptk's—sun-colored and healthy. She carried a long spear of hemlock wood, perfectly sized as a walking stick, charred, smoothed, and treated often with tallow on one end. Fitted with an obsidian blade—three fingers wide, a hand long, and a whole thumb thick—hers was the finest spear anyone in her family band could remember seeing."

Seesterfekt pauses and looks at me. "Did you know Ankit-ip traded an entire stag-moose hide with a family band far to the west for the obsidian to make that blade?"

"Uh, no, I didn't."

"She was also the first human to tie locks of woolly mammoth hair to her spear to dampen the sound of it being used as a walking stick," Seest says, laughing. "She was right. A dead stick makes a completely different sound than a live one when you hit it. And the animals she hunted knew this very well."

"How did Ankit-ip get the woolly mammoth hair?"

"Hunting, of course."

Surrounding it... it's huge... spears and rocks... is that enough?

"Surrounding it?" Seest says. "Didn't I say earlier that humans back then weren't ignorant brutes?"

"Yes, well, I mean, isn't that how they hunted them?" I say, sheepishly defending my museum memory.

Seesterfekt's eyes grow like rapidly filling balloons. Bellows of laughter echo through the woods. "That's the way museum manikins hunt them," Seest says, barely able to get the words out before bursting into laughter again.

"I don't know," I say, shrugging.

"But I do know, don't I?" Seest says, with an opposite-eye-bulging wink. Seest places another stick on the glowing embers. "Do you think humans were stupid enough to try to kill something the size of a woolly mammoth on foot? They used horses."

I'm dumbfounded.

"Your paleontologist's conjecture, supported by archeological evidence of butchered horses, claims that humans hunted them. But eating them was a common practice when horses were no longer useful. And that's not the only time horses were butchered. When several family bands forged an alliance, they'd claim and protect a hunting and gathering territory. These unified bands—often considered a single band—aggressively attacked any intruders. But few if any humans killed each other during these attacks. Instead, the unified bands positioned themselves to gain advantage over the intruders."

"I'm not sure I follow. What do you mean by *positioned themselves*?"

"In those days, when humans claimed a territory, it was understood that they knew it so well—the animals, the vegetation, the terrain, the rivers and lakes—that no one else could possibly succeed in out maneuvering them there. 'Positioning' was a way for the unified band to display their territorial right by trapping the intruders in a canyon, or against a mountain, in the oxbow of a river—any natural feature that made it impossible to escape without direct confrontation with the unified band."

"Fascinating."

"Yes, and confrontation was considered an unforgivable act of aggression, since the intruders were already violating a territorial claim just by being there."

"An unforgivable act of aggression? What does that mean? And how could they escape without a confrontation if they were trapped?"

"An unforgivable act of aggression drew an immediate death sentence for the intruders. But intruders had a survivable alternative against overwhelming odds from the unified band whose territory was breached."

"Go on."

"If the intruders yielded, the unified band killed the intruder's horses to secure their advantage over them. It was then customary and considered good manners to butcher the horses and give the meat to the defeated as an act of neutrality. The idea wasn't to starve the intruders to death, just drive them away. Meat from the butchered horses insured their survival while they searched for other places to hunt and gather. And always, a horse or two was spared to carry the dried meat. Horses were a means to an end, and that end was securing territory and food and driving others away."

I'm beginning to understand the reason woolly mammoths declined after that period.

"Yes," Seesterfekt says, shaking head 'no.' "You're beginning to see from that point on. But what you don't see is the time before that period when more mammoths and mastodons were migrating to North America from Asia than at any other time."

"Why?"

"Overhunting in Asia by former rhino skin traders."

"They used horses also?"

"Yes, of course," Seest says. "They had already pushed the rhinos near extinction. And they were demanding too high of a price for skins—wives, daughters, sons, entire families in some cases. With humans in North America unwilling to trade such things, the rhino traders stopped bringing skins here, staying in Asia where a few buyers at any price could be found. But after the last viable animals were hunted, rhino skin traders began hunting mammoths and mastodons, driving more and more of them into North America. This is when the real trouble began between unified bands and large companies of traders. These unified bands aligned with other unified bands, uniting into tribes big enough to drive off the traders who were now hunting these animals in the tribes' combined territories. And driving off traders didn't call for manners or acts of neutrality, my friend. It called for merciless savagery, which was exacted on them without hesitation."

Solemn and reflective, Seesterfekt stares at faint tree shadows—cast by the light of Jupiter overhead—on patches of night-white snow.

As fascinating as all of this is, why doesn't it surprise me... humans, territory, trade, conflict... nothing's changed...

gurgling stream... flickering fire... soothing... what about Ankit-ip...

"What? Ah yes, Anki," Seesterfekt says, eyes glinting. "She was bright, intuitive, and brave. Rather than returning home that day, Ankit-ip made a fire and stayed the night in the highlands. No easy task since fuelwood for an extended fire wasn't readily available there. But she maintained a smolder through the night with enough heat to keep her from freezing. And from it, she used charcoal and ash to treat her breechclout and hide her scent."

"So I'm assuming you joined her at the fire."

"Of course. As you now know, I can't pass up a good fire. Ankit-ip was expecting me. She'd heard that the Peepl lived in the highlands and went there hoping to meet one. She wasn't expecting the cat though, and thanked me for suggesting the animal go away."

"How did she know you suggested that?"

"She didn't know that. Not for certain. But she'd heard through stories that the Peepl could suggest alternate behavior in animals. That's why she ran toward me."

"An act of faith? Or hope?"

"At that moment? Desperation." Seesterfekt laughs. "Ankit-ip was a wise and competent woman of her family band. Faith wasn't part of her life. Neither was hope. Believing nothing, she was content with everything. Content with everything, she hoped for nothing. I've never met another human like her in all my wanderings."

"I'm not a student of it, but why does Buddhism come to mind?"

Seesterfekt looks off into the dark woods, again whistling the fluty notes of a hermit thrush.

Nope, I'm not biting. No way.

"Suit yourself," Seest says, shrugging. "Trading was Anki-ip's strong point. She built friendships with several family bands living in the same watershed who traded with bands from the big mountains in the west, to the end of land in the east, and beyond the warmth of always summer in the south."

"And north?"

"Ankit-ip's band were all from there, moving further north with their growing families as the ice retreated. She was an influential negotiator, striking agreements between northern and southern bands allowing enough animals to pass, unmolested from south to north, in established corridors where hunting was forbidden. This maintained populations in the north, while still ensuring enough resources for bands in the south, whose populations grew faster than the northern bands. It took a lot of cooperation between families to do this, the most vulnerable being those of the north. But they were also the most hardy and quickest to answer violations of standing agreements. And by *maintained populations*, I mean plants and animals first, and humans second. This was no hokey rhetoric, my friend," Seest says. "This was acceptance of the fact that human health depends on the health of everything else. Another good idea long forgotten."

"I'm amazed again that humans were practicing conservation twelve thousand years ago."

"And good politics," Seest says with a wink and nod. "It was a workable arrangement that lasted for thousands of years as the glaciers retreated at a faster rate than they ever have."

"Even now?" I ask.

"Now is nothing." Seest laughs. "There's hardly any ice left to melt!

"Ankit-ip never gave birth or chose a mate. Customary gender-role partnering just didn't interest her, and because of that she was rumored to favor females. But she favored neither females nor males, this I saw many times. She was as restless in this respect as in any other."

"I don't get it. Ankit-ip was restless, yet content with everything?"

"As I said before, I've never known another human like her. If you met her, you'd understand. We wandered for many years, and as with humans I'd befriended before her, Ankit-ip retold stories of the Peepl to whomever she met until, in her forty-third year, she died from a snake bite while relieving herself in the predawn darkness."

"That's hard to believe. Was it a common occurrence?"

"No," Seest says. "The day before was hot and dry, and that night, the temperature dropped fast. The rattlesnake she stepped on never rattled. She didn't feel the slow bite on her half-frozen foot or realize the snake was attached to her until she moved. Ankit-ip worked fast, carefully prying open the snake's mouth with her knife, then cutting her foot to bleed out the poison. She was calm. She'd been bitten before. But too much venom had entered her bloodstream and she knew it. Ankit-ip died with dignity, sitting quiet, accepting her moment till she slumped over, dead. This is when I began my last Faabl sit long, twelve thousand twelve years ago."

Seesterfekt vanishes through the blue-orange flicker and night-cloaked smoke of our fading fire. I feel the absence of a dear friend and realize, through story, Seesterfekt said goodbye before leaving.

"Safe travels, my friend," come Seest's parting words through the distance of darkened woods.

Driving in the left lane of a twisting sun-baked Saint Lucian highway, I long for the snow-covered mountain roads of Winhall, Vermont. At least there you can count on people driving on the right side of the road.

Chapter 13

On The Southern Pillar

April 29 2018
Full Moon

Fifth Whole Moon

Five kilometers from Hewanorra Airport, while fighting with the air conditioner that just quit, I make a wrong turn and end up in a place called Londonderry. I'm reminded to be careful what I wish for. Back home, Londonderry is one of the towns adjacent to Winhall, but on this lonely stretch of road along a soft ridgeline, fenced in on both sides with vegetation, there's nothing that remotely resembles "town." It's not a total waste though. From here, I have the first glimpse of my destination nearly nine kilometers away—as the Carib grackle flies. The Southern Pillar, as Seesterfekt calls it: Gros Piton.

Heading northwest after returning to the highway, ever-changing views of island and sea open and close as the road snakes its way along the coast. After passing through the town of Choiseul, the road turns north. Then southwest. Then northeast... northwest... south... northwest... southwest... I can't remember which side of the road to stay on.

Reaching La Pointe, I turn right and drive inland on a gentle uphill grade. The road is fairly straight. Now that there's blood flowing through my knuckles again, I can relax a bit and enjoy the drive.

What will I say? ...doesn't matter... Tsitsyoos will know what I'm thinking anyway... At least he'll know I'm coming... 'he'? ... yes... Koodj... not past the age of gender... what does he have for me? ...why me? ...aren't there other peop—shit—humans here to give it to?

Thick roadside vegetation narrows the byway as I drive down a steep grade. At the bottom of the hill, the pavement ends at a small stream where a dirt road continues on, widening unevenly. Small signs appear announcing the arrival at my destination: Gros Piton Nature Trail.

Cool, moist air envelopes me as I squeeze out of the mobile sauna I paid for, thinking it was a rental car. Trees, bushes, and plants, entangled from ground to canopy, create an impenetrable, multi-tiered forest. Maintained views—for the benefit of tourists—reveal Gros Piton's foreboding sheer rock walls below jutting vegetation that wreathes this ancient volcanic cone.

Wait... what if I know too much?... an accident they'll say... a man died... he slipped and fell off a cliff at Gros Piton... no, come on...

Following signs to the trailhead through the tiny hamlet of Fond Gens Libre, my anxiety loosens its grip. When I arrive at the Gros Piton Nature Trail Interpretive Center, it clamps down again. I have to enlist the services of a guide. No one is allowed to hike here alone. As if that isn't bad enough news, the last hike leaves at 14:00, two and a half hours ago.

Now what? Seest said I had to be there today.

Walking back through the village, I hear familiar bird notes and phrases, similar to those of migrating birds that are now arriving in the forests at home. It's a welcome distraction from my current predicament. A winter-wren-sounding-twinkle weaves through cocoa tree leaves as I near the car. I see it: a warbler with bright yellow neck, breast, and underbelly, and a black eye line.

"Èske w renmen wabla Sent Lisi nou an?"

I look into the thick jungle cover for whoever belongs to the voice. No one's there. "I'm sorry?"

"Yoa like hour Saint Looshian wahblah?" the voice says, as a young woman emerges from the forest. "Mwen wè ou renmen zwazo?"

"I like the Saint Lucian warbler, yes. But I don't understand creole. I'm sorry."

"Yoa like di bawds?"

"Yes, I do."

"Yoa like di people?"

"Sometimes."

"Yoa like di Peepl wit di fehdaz?"

Don't answer... Who is this?... She doesn't seem threatening.

"If I waz tretennin', yoa would knowit by now," my new acquaintance says, bursting into laughter.

Hell of a coincidence... my last thought... what she just said.

Motioning me closer with her index finger, head tilted down, eyes peering up from just below her brow, she whispers, "Koodj Tsitsyoos?"

Our noses nearly touch.

Her eyes are black, her skin, a rich dark brown—somewhere between cinnamon and mocha. A glistening, onyx mane of voluminous hair, pulled back tight, frames her attractive face, a face soft with the vitality of youth, yet hard as though forged in the rigors of experience. I give her my best you-don't-scare-me look.

Recoiling, with legs and feet fixed, she smiles. "Yoa doan skayhr me eadah, mistah."

Another coincidence?

She steps back. "Yoa ahr ok," she says, still smiling. "Yoa I will tek, dough I yahm doudful yoa'll suhvive."

Still unsure about her... what does she mean?... you I will take, though I am doubtful you'll survive... Caribbean English... Saint Lucian Creole... wait... what's that patch on her shirt? Shit... she's a guide... that's what she meant...she'll take me... but doubtful I'll surv—

"Yoa wanna go or note?" she says.

"But the last hike left at 14:00."

"Dènye pwomnad, wi, men sa pa yon pwomnad, sa se yon entwodiksyon. Byenvini nan vale moun ki lib."

"I don't know what you're saying."

"Yoa doan know anyting, do yoa?! Di lass hike, yea, butdis iz note a hike, dis iz ahn introduckshiahn. Welcome to di Volley ov di Free Peepl," she says, motioning me to follow.

Valley of the Free Peepl…. Fond Gens Libre… ugh, what an idiot, of course.

"Yehs, Ole Purbit tellin' yoa."

Is she reading my thoughts? "What's your name?"

"No names! Nehvah repeat names. Yoa'ahr new aht dis."

I'm humbled by my ignorance.

"Li bon lè yon moun emb."

"I'm sorry, what did you say?"

"Li bon lè yon moun emb. Humbled iz good."

"Ok, stop!" I bark, halting in front of the Interpretive Center.

"Note heah," she whispers with absolute authority, while continuing on her way. "Or we ahr doan."

Entering a forested boulder field just beyond the last building on the gentle approach to the Gros Piton trail, my guide finally stops. "Wot do yoa wanna say?"

"How did you know what I was thinking back there?"

"I yahm note yoar Teacha. Purbit iz. Ahsk dat ole Seestahfekt when yoa get bach home," she says with a big smile, turning and continuing up the trail. "Or maybe yoa'ahr goinda find out tonight." She laughs.

Tonight?...

A large flycatcher sits on a branch, watching me as I pass underneath it. Twice the size of any flycatcher in Vermont, its creamy yellow breast reflects the dappled sunlight sifting through forest understory.

"Lessah Ahntillian. Big flycatcha," my guide says, dashing along, quickly gaining elevation where the canopy opens for a view south toward the island of Saint Vincent. "Di day iz growin' ole, like yoa," she says, giggling from a few meters ahead.

. . .

At a magnificent viewpoint of Petit Piton rising from the sea, a clear-voiced bird sings from below the trail.

Is that a house wren?

"Yoa'ahr right; di bawd yoa heah iz cōmanly known az di house wren, but soon gettin' reckonishon az ah distink species."

She IS reading my thoughts... wait... is that a broad-winged hawk?

"Yoa really like di bawds," my much younger companion says, walking a steep incline at a much younger pace than I. "It iz di broahdwing."

. . .

She stops for a moment at what resembles an avalanche gully with unobstructed views extending all the way down to the ocean. "Roak slide," she says. "Dis iz di ahfway point."

Halfway... great...

Picking up the pace in a relatively flat section of trail beyond the gully, she waves for me to move faster. "Wot iz greaht iz dat yoa hahv note died yet," she says, laughing.

"Yes," is all I can mutter while trying to keep up. *But stop reading my thoughts.*

. . .

Benches at the base of a huge mango tree stare at me with pity as I walk by, obeying my taskmaster's request while she continues up trail. "Doan worry aboud yoar tawts, dare ahr othah dings to worry aboud."

. . .

Sweat-soaked and thirsty, I plod along as the trail ascends in a near vertical hodgepodge of rock and root stairs. There's an opening up ahead, but no sign of my guide.

Shit, did she fall off one of those cliffs I saw from the car?

"Ok yoa," she barks, handing me a bottle of water as I emerge out of the jungle cover onto bare rock at the summit. "I broad yoa heah and I be bach foah yoa in di moahnin'."

"Wait-wait-wait. Tomorrow?"

"Ou wè solèy sa lòt bò a mesye? L'ap kouche, Mwen prale, bòn chans pou aswè a."

"Enough with the god-damned creole!"

"Yoa see dat sun ovah dare mistah," she says, pointing west with one arm. "It's settin', I yahm leavin'."

Frozen in place, I watch her disappear through the jungle below.

What do I do? Shit... I'm not prepared for this... What am I doing here? What was I thinking?

"Yoa'll suhvive. Maybe," Ms. leave-me-here-to-die says, her voice fading, already many meters down the trail.

"Seesterfekt Purbits, what did you talk me into?" I say, looking up at the sky.

A blood red moon captivates me, rising between lush green hills and the gold Caribbean sunset reflecting off clouds over Mount Gimie.

"Purbits is here?" a non-gendered voice says from thick foliage rustling to my right.

A brindle bundle of feather-hair rolls out of the vegetation.

"I am Koodj Tsitsyoos," the bundle says, standing upright.

Looks like a brindle Seesterfekt.

"You can call me Koodj, Tsitsyoos, Tsits... Seesterfekt Purbits is here?" Koodj says, looking around.

"No, just me, the lone *sapiens*," I say, deadpan.

Tsitsyoos giggles a hearty Peepl giggle then, pointing toward the moon low in the east, collapses.

What's that scent? Keysha... Dominique... Lisa... ah, Lisa... she could really... wait... why am I thinking of my high school girlfriends?

"Koodj, Koodj," I whisper.

Sitting up, Koodj Tsitsyoos looks deep into my eyes. "It is starting."

"What's starting?"

"The molt."

Jumping to my feet, eyes wide open, I realize what that scent was. "You're female?!"

"Yes, well, last time I looked."

"Looked?! What do you mean, looked? I thought you had your sex with feathers," I say, knowing this sounds wrong as I speak it.

"Why, do you?"

"We don't have sex with feathers."

"I have heard of it," Tsitsyoos says, giggling.

"Ok, stop. I understood you were male."

"Yes, I know," she says. "Seesterfekt never explained it, the way to know from our chosen names."

"I have no idea what you're talking about. I'm sorry."

"Beginning in Koodj and ending with the onset of Manthasif, the last sound in our chosen name identifies our gender. Tsitsyoo is my chosen name and 's' at the end denotes my gender as female. It's the same with Seesterfekt Purbits."

My jaw drops. "Seesterfekt Purbits is female?!"

"Was female." Tsitsyoos laughs. "Big surprise for you, yes? You are such a gender-head."

"But she, he, ugh! Whatever... told me that during the molt, they lay with a female."

"Yes, and, was there a bulb from the union?"

"Uh, hmm."

"No," she says. "There was not. That is not what happened..."

Her voice is spellbinding.

"...Koodj Purbits was female. She lay with another female because there were no males suitable for molting when her time came—only one other female: Koodj Wookwahs.

"This is not something forbidden, different, or unusual among the Peepl, as humans perceive it to be for themselves from time to time and place to place throughout your history. Like-genders molt together by choice, or when there are no suitable opposites available. Those who resist lying with the same gender, thinking they can pass through the molt on their own, almost always die from predation because one of the Peepl alone does not have enough strength of domain to protect themselves while molting. Of course, no bulbs result from the union, but the odds of surviving increase exponentially. Predation of the Peepl has always been a danger because of very strong pheromones produced at molting. These are extremely attractive to mammals—particularly humans."

My fairy dust moment dissolves. "So why am I here? Seesterfekt said you have something for me?"

"Maybe I do and maybe I do not," Tsitsyoos says. "But you are here to protect me since there are no Koodj left who are suitable for molting."

"But I thought contact with humans was forbidden as Koodj."

"It was, and still is, traditionally. Seesterfekt Purbits was the first to break with—"

"Yes, I've heard some of Seesterfekt's stories and the results of veering from the tradition of The Forbidden. There was good reason for that rule."

"With so few of us left it is a pointless limitation."

In the west, sunset hides beyond the sea, shadowing skies above. Though the moon, high in the east, resists the dark.

"And your sensory domain? It's expanded also?" I say, remembering what Seesterfekt said about the normal reach of a Koodj's sensory domain being a thousand kilometers.

"Yes, Seesterfekt Purbits has been my teacher via sensory domain since my emergence."

"Your sensory domain reached that far at emergence?"

Looking into my eyes, Tsitsyoos collapses again. By the light of the full moon, Koodj Tsitsyoos' coat is the most beautiful thing I've ever seen.

That scent... mmm, Lisa... heart pounding... wait a minute... "No-no-no!"

Tsits recovers consciousness at my barking.

"Is this what you have for me? What about that nice young woman who led me up here, can't she—"

"Shh," Tsitsyoos whispers. "She has done this already, right in this very place, years ago, with Koodj Khetchishsht. It will be alright. You must protect me from predators. That is all. If we both survive, in the morning you will have a better understanding."

"If we both survive?!"

"Shh."

"Survive what?" I whisper.

"Sit here where these rocks form a seat with a backrest," she says, walking to an arrangement of rocks.

Not bad... comfortable... still warm from the sun...

Koodj Tsitsyoos crawls onto my lap and gazes into my eyes. It's provocative, uncomfortable.

"Thank you," she says, pushing her body against my chest the way a cat does when asking if it can stay a while.

As I stroke her head, she curls up and falls asleep.

Eight hundred meters above the sea... in the jungle atop an extinct volcanic dome... three-thousand-year-old female-soon-to-be-non-gendered Peepl in my lap... come-and-get-me scent is enough to wake up the dead... cacophony of dog song in the valley below... little water... no food... no weapon... no communication... shit... not good... uncomfortable... the rocks are cooling...

A beautiful chorus of insect and frog song fills the jungle. It's a mellifluous foreground to a transiting full moon reflecting off the sea in the west and mountains in the east. Shadows on the edge of jungle play tricks with my mind. The distinct sound of purring from Koodj Tsitsyoos, asleep on my lap, replaces dog song, now silent in the valley.

They purr... Seesterfekt didn't tell me... female, huh? Old Purbits was female... my propensity for preconception paints everything... shadows and sound moving through the jungle... what happened to the insect and frog song? Shit... the shadows have eyes... they're everywhere...

...

Be still?

...

Kitties?

...

Why am I having a conversation with myself about kitties?

...

It's you, Koodj?

...

They're your kitties?

...

Wait, how are you able to do this, aren't humans unaffected by the domain of impelment?

...

You've been working on it? Great, when were you going to tell me?

...

Ok, ok, so the cats are here to help?

...

Not cats? I thought you said kitties.

...

RATS?!

...

Saint Lucia giant rice rat believed to be extinct since the mid eighteen hundreds?

...

Yes, very cute, you've said. They're your kitties, but what are these cat-sized rats here to help with?

...

What other mammals?

The arrival of dozens of panting dogs and a horde of large bats circling over Gros Piton in a slow, funnel-forming cloud disrupts my in-head conversation.

The bats wouldn't happen to be your kitties, too, would they?

...

Spectral bats, indigenous to the Antilles. Very nice, but are they yours?

...

No, I didn't think so.

...

Don't move? Why?

...

The rats will devour me? Oh, good, thanks for the advice.

...

Why would I want to close my eyes?

Instantly, the funnel cloud of bats descends toward the summit. Dozens of dogs lunge at Koodj and I. An immeasurable number of rats leap from the jungle cover, filling the sky and covering the ground around us.

Don't move, Koodj said, don't move...

. . .

Shrieking, growling, screaming, and a sound like thick, wet canvas tearing—slabs of flesh, ripped from the bone—echo through the mountains. The air fills with the smell of raw meat. Eviscerated dogs spatter on the ground like the fat raindrops that fall just before a downpour. Flailing bats, pulled from the sky, burst open as leaping rats tear at their bodies from every direction. Blood-mist turns the moonlight red. Tremors grip me...

. . .

As instantly as it began, the onslaught ends.

In the potent white moonlight, Tsitsyoos' 'kitties' scurry about, consuming and removing the carnage. Not knowing if it's safe yet, I continue my vigilant stillness.

In my lap, Koodj lies curled up, asleep, surrounded by a brindle wreath of shed feather-hair. Her exposed black skin glistens in the moonlight.

My eyes grow heavy as I gaze out over the water. The chorus of insect and frog song resumes, drowning out the other sounds around us. I nod off... My head snaps to attention, my eyes spring open. I nod off again... My head snaps to attention, but this time, my eyes won't open. I'm exhausted. I give in and fall deep asleep.

. . .

"Ki kote Seestahgohd Tsitsyoos?"

Huh? Oh... I'm dreaming.

"WEAHR IZ TSITSYOOS?!"

Shit! It's not a dream!

I fling open my eyes. My nameless guide hovers over me like a giant hornet about to sting.

"You can't believe what happened here last night," I say, looking down at my lap, seeing nothing but the dried scant remains of brindle sheddings.

"NovishiAt!" she snaps. "I know wot hopponed heah. I wanna know WEAHR IZ TSITSYOOS?"

“I’m here,” a giggling feminine voice calls from below us.

I rush blindly through the thick vegetation toward Tsitsyoos.

What is she yelling stop? We’ve found Tsits… What’s the problem… Oh SHIT!

My guide grabs me from behind as I break through the vegetation at a cliff edge. “Yehs! Dis iz why I waz yehlin’ to stohp! LOOK DARE!” She says, pointing at Tsitsyoos plunging through the canopy below.

Part Three

A Changing Reality

The jeweled midnight sky casts faint tree shadows on the rocks around me. Though just beginning to open, leaves of the surrounding deciduous forest hush the swirling breeze atop my mini piton back in Winhall, two weeks after arriving home from Saint Lucia.

Chapter 14

While Waiting

May 15, 2018
New Moon

Fifth Day Moon
In the wee-est of hours

Still no sign of Seesterfekt Purbits anywhere in the forest.

"No sign?" Seesterfekt materializes in the starlight. "You want I should leave a sign?"

"Female?! Really! Why weren't you more specific?"

"What's the difference? And why didn't you pay closer attention instead of allowing your infantile, gender-based human preconception to color my words?" Seest grins widely.

"And what's this about you being my teacher?"

"I thought that was obvious," Seest says, gesturing with a hand the way Grandma Ida used to— thumb, index, and middle finger held tight at their tips, hinged wrist flopping toward and away from her face.

"I suppose it is." I laugh. "It's good to see you, Teacher. How long have you been here?"

"Since the thirtieth."

"What? Why? How could you know I'd be coming here? I've never climbed this knob before. I didn't even think of it till this morning after giving up on trying to find you. How could you have known on April thirtieth I'd be coming here tonight?"

"Tsitsyoos," Seest says.

"Tsitsyoos?! Listen... You and I have a lot to talk abou—"

Seesterfekt raises a hand. "Yes we do. Sit, let's talk while we wait."

"Wait for what?"

"Let's talk about Koodj," Seest says.

"Koodj? You mean Seestergohd, Seestergohd Tsitsyoos?"

"No my friend, I mean Koodj—not past the age of gender."

"I don't really have two thousand years to spare."

"Well, how about enough time to hear a little natural history from my early Koodj years?"

Resigning myself, I put aside memories of Saint Lucia, and get comfortable among the rocks.

Seesterfekt takes a deep breath. "I went from my last Faabl sit long to my first Koodj sit long, 11,999 years ago. Incidentally, I was full grown at that point, having been stunted earlier by being bulb for so long."

"You sat for twenty-six years?"

"Yes, but with a short break to stretch my legs." Seest laughs. "I left my far northern last Faabl sit long place and traveled south for a lunation, arriving at an area where mixed-wood forests grew beneath massive white pine trees hundreds of meters apart. It was there that I decided to stay for my first Koodj sit long. You see, Koodj is the formative years with everything that grows and multiplies, be it plant or animal, single-celled or very large."

"Compared to the formative years with rock, water, and wind, I imagine that would be much more complicated."

"It is. Indeed it is. Mastodons lived in the area, feasting on the understory for kilometers in every direction. Winters were short and mild, and summers were long, dry, and increasingly warm. However, near the end of that sit long, everything changed."

A soft breeze, hushed by infant leaves chills the wee-hour air.

"I was fortunate to have sat long there," Seest says. "It was on a high plateau about four kilometers northwest of what is now called Table Rock Mountain, just south of your North and South Carolina borders. In those days the humans who lived nearby called it Angakhemechehehposh."

"That's a mouthful."

"It means Where the Big Ones Fight. But your language is so abbreviated that place names like this are irrelevant. My story has so many place names that you'd be lost if I used them, so I'll use the names that are relevant to your time."

"That's probably best, thank you."

Seesterfekt nods, peering into the darkened woods.

"Everything alright?"

"Yes, yes, of course." Seest brushes off my question with flick of the wrist. "The southern herd of the eastern mastodons by that time was dwindling. Small pods from what are now central Ohio and northern Kentucky, where browse was scarce, began roaming with the southern herd. They were welcome additions. But even with these, the southern herd didn't match the total number of individuals from the northern herd.

"The drying climate and hunting pressure from humans, and what your science calls dire wolfs, was intense in the south. The territory that supported the mastodons was quickly shrinking. Your Appalachian Mountains from what you've named the Chattahoochee National Forest in the south, up to your Cherokee National Forest in the north, was their last refuge.

"It's very different now than when I sat long there. Back then, Angakhemechehehposh was a revered monolith where mastodons gathered to sun themselves in winter and establish mating rights in spring.

"In those days, no humans hunted the highlands north of the Oolenoy River, and south of the Bursted Rock Creek. Many streams and rivers east and west of the highlands completed this boundary. It was about one hundred sixty-eight square kilometers. Forty-one thousand acres in total. These were the lands of the southern herds of the eastern mastodons and Angakhemechehehposh sat almost centered there." Seesterfekt laughs. "But the Oolenoy was a favorite gathering place for the mastodons, and it used to frustrate the humans who camped nearby who could neither kill the animals because of their agreements with other bands, nor use the river for fresh water when the mastodon were present. Sometimes an entire lunation would pass before the mastodon would leave the Oolenoy's wide, deep waters."

"Yuk. The water must have been disgusting for a while after they left."

Seest laughs harder. "It wasn't the river so much. The Oolenoy was part of a large enough watershed that a good regional rain would wash it clean. But the surrounding banks and forests where the mastodon gathered were trampled, stripped bare, and left covered in mastodon poo."

We laugh together while I imagine the reactions of humans living in the area during a mastodon invasion.

"The northern herds," Seest says, still smiling, "of the eastern mastodons at that time, browsed a territory whose northern border extended along your Mohawk River, from what you call Schoharie Creek in the west, to your Hudson River in the east. Squeezing south past the east wall of what are now the Catskill Mountains and widening again, the western border extended to the confluence of your Delaware and Neversink Rivers. The southern boarder stretched from that confluence, eastward, back to the Hudson at what's known as Moodna Creek, via the area of what is now Warwick, New York. This territory was also about forty-one thousand acres."

"Any mastodon invasions of human camps along these rivers?"

"No. Humans in the north seemed to avoid the areas along the favorite rivers of the mastodon, always camping kilometers upstream of these places. And especially so where the northern herd gathered annually in the narrow area of land between the Catskills and the Hudson to socialize and choose mates." Seesterfekt laughs. "Some of those poor mastodon whose pod wouldn't allow it for the present season would betroth themselves for the next season."

"Wait—what? Imposing pachyderms? Affianced elephants? Come on Purbits, really?"

"No. Elephants don't affiance themselves. Neither did woollys, or any mastodons other than those of the northern herd from the east. But sadder than the sting of unrequited love, was the fact that—even though no humans hunted them several lunations before the annual gathering, having come to a similar agreement as their southern neighbors—soon after the mastodons paired up and began mating, it was declared open season on any unmated males, breeding age or older. This, of course, often made keeping the promise of betrothal impossible."

"You're serious, aren't you? I mean about the betrothals."

"Yes, very, and the custom of killing breeding-age males took its toll on the mastodon population. It had become somewhat of a contest to see which human family could procure the most meat and skins immediately following the annual gathering. It was unwise to kill young males every year. Many of them would have eventually grown into ideal progenitors."

Seesterfekt stares off into the night-blackened forest.

"I don't get it," I say. "Earlier humans were practicing conservation. Why didn't this generation follow their example? Wasn't that information handed down?"

"Humans have volumes of history handed down and still repeat it. Why does this particular instance surprise you?"

Don't really know... suppose it shouldn't...

"No wisdom gained is guarantee it'll be used once those who gain it are gone," Seest says.

"But this isn't the change at the end of your first Koodj sit long that you mentioned, is it?"

"No, it's not," Seest says, with a headshake. "When the body of glacial water your geologists call Lake Vermont breached its barrier where the Hudson River now flows east out of the mountains, the water rushed south in a cataclysmic flood, reshaping your Hudson Valley. Everything washed into the sea from sixty kilometers north of present-day Albany to the outlet of floodwater in the south past your New York City. Evidence of it remains in trenches and boulders on the ocean floor, all the way out to the continental shelf almost two hundred kilometers offshore. Draining quickly, the lake began siphoning fresh water out from under the adjacent continental glacier your scientists call the Laurentide ice sheet. Immense air pockets, compressed by seawater rushing from the Atlantic into what is now the Saint Lawrence Valley, pushed up on the underside of the glacier, creating fissures before fiercely backwashing into the Atlantic. This produced a low-frequency vibration throughout, causing the great sheet to quake. From this, and the absence of support from fresh water already drained out, weak layers of the ice sheet collapsed, blocking the flow of fresh water that was siphoning south."

"Weak layers of the ice sheet?"

"Yes, weakened by the asteroid and comet debris five hundred years earlier. "

"Right. While you were still bulb."

"Yes." Seesterfekt nods. "The sudden blockage of water flowing south under the ice created a seiche wave lasting a few days, mixing salt water with fresh, creating the brackish body of water your science calls the Champlain Sea. But the quaking Laurentide ice sheet caused tremors on the ground and even greater seiche waves in the largest glacial lake on the continent at that time; the one your geologists call Lake Agassiz. Breaching the terminal moraine that once held it back at a high point of land in the northeast corner of your South Dakota that now divides the Hudson's Bay's watershed from the Gulf of Mexico's, Lake Agassiz drained through the cataclysm you refer to as the Glacial River Warren while floodwaters in the east drained the Hudson Valley. The force of the flood in your Mississippi Valley was so great that evidence of it remains in a massive debris plain in the Gulf of Mexico, sloping into the depths, two hundred kilometers offshore."

"I'm familiar with these two events, but I thought they occurred at different times, separated by thousands of years?"

"Yes, that's what is thought to have happened." Seesterfekt looks toward Mars, Saturn, and Jupiter, low in the southern sky. "But that's incorrect. One triggered the other."

Dawn is near... hmm... not tired.

"Good, because I'm not finished," Seest says.

Will I ever have another thought without you knowing what it is?

"You sure you're not tired? You're thinking like you're tired."

No, actually that was a deliberate, baited thought. So, will I?

"Will you what?"

Ok, you win. I'm too tired for this.

"Yes, I know. I said you were tired. May I continue?"

Ugh! "Yes, please, anything. Just stop going on about this."

"The northern mastodons, caught between the Hudson River and the Catskill Mountains, faced a roiling brown wall of water and debris over one hundred meters high. A few crossed the river east before it arrived, but they were eventually swept off the lowlands on the other side.

"A small number of stragglers to the gathering reached what you call Shunnemunk Mountain before the floodwaters rose there. After the water receded, they traveled southwest, meeting up with a group that managed to survive the periphery of the flood. But all thirteen died soon after from exhaustion, in an area roughly centered on both sides of your present-day New York, New Jersey border. In the meantime, dozens of unpaired individual mastodons traveled up what's known now as Esopus Creek to the west side of your Slide Mountain. From there they journeyed to the west branch of the Neversink River, following it to the Delaware River—the border of their territory. Continuing along the northern high ground of the geologic fault crease in Pennsylvania to the Frankstown area, then traveling along the western edge of the Appalachian Mountains to the area of Saltville, Virginia, they passed through what is famously known as the Gray fossil site in Tennessee, on to the Tuckaleechee caverns area, finally arriving at Angakhemechehehposh: Table Rock Mountain in South Carolina. The truth is, few made it there. Most died along the way from exhaustion and despair, leaving a trail of bones for your science to piece their story together."

“You were with those who escaped the flood, weren’t you?”

“Yes, I was. I was there in the northern breeding lands when the floodwaters roared down the Hudson Valley. I suggested as many as possible hurry up the gorge, but panic struck and they stampeded the entrance. Many were lost. It was sad, my friend, to watch such large animals wash away like ants in a rainstorm.”

“I’m confused. I thought your first Koodj sit long was near Angakhemechehehposh, where you began this story.”

“You’re the first human in ten thousand years to pronounce that properly! But yes, it’s true. My story began there. Immediately following my first Koodj sit long, I traveled to the narrows to be part of the annual meeting of the northern herd.”

“Were you looking for a mate?”

“Yes, but none of them could handle me.” Seesterfekt grins.

“This time frame, these cataclysms, this was twelve thousand years ago?”

“Eleven thousand nine hundred eighty-six. A few lunations after my first Koodj sit long.” Seest again peers into the darkness.

“If you don’t mind me asking, what’s the point of all this?”

"The point?" Seest laughs. "Everything I tell you is true. Some accounts, like those of Ptk and Ankit-ip can never be substantiated with evidence. But with these accounts my friend, evidence exists, if you're willing to look outside the box, as you call it, of your present preconceptions. Now, where was I?...

"Ah, yes. The raging floodwaters in the Mississippi Valley triggered an eastward exodus of lowland mastodon herds toward Angakhemechehehposh. Small pods from what are western Mississippi and eastern Missouri escaped across the lowlands before the floodwaters arrived, but a large pod from the area of northeastern Arkansas drowned trying to cross east against the torrent. Other pods came to Angakhemechehehposh from the south and east: western Alabama, northern Florida, southern South Carolina, and northern North Carolina."

"Angakhemechehehposh must have been paradise to those that made it there."

"Except that there were predators—the big toothed cats, dire wolfs, and giant short-face bear—in pursuit of the mastodons, now the largest, most plentiful land prey available, since any horses not consumed by the flood had migrated to the open plains west of the inundated Mississippi Valley."

"But with all the carnage left behind by the floods, wouldn't any of those predators have been satisfied with an easy meal rather than having to bring down a mastodon?"

"Yes, excellent thought, one which the predators themselves had right away. But try telling that to a flock of vultures who can find and claim every worthwhile carcass easier and faster than you."

"Vultures? Come on Purbits, vultures are no match for the predators you mentioned."

"With wingspans of four meters and a weight of twenty kilos, a flock of a dozen or more of what your science has named *Teratornis merriami* were too formidable for any predator of that time, even packs of dire wolfs."

"I had no idea."

"No, you didn't. And you didn't know that humans in the area at that time called them Etōchawuk Chadōh."

"Meaning?"

"Winged Corpse Eater."

"That's pleasant."

"It's the one moment in all my memories of them when they didn't accompany large predators following migrating herds of prey. They had food to last for many months as a result of the receding floodwaters. It was the height of their existence on this continent: a breath in time. But it was also the beginning of an existence of persecution, as humans turned their grief to hatred. Gliding on four-meter wingspans, they became daily reminders of death and decay, shadows that searched from above for their next victims. It didn't matter that what they searched for was dead already, superstition blossoms during disaster, and unfortunately, vultures became despised and feared as omens."

Darkness... despair... anger...

"Those aren't my feelings my friend," Seesterfekt says, "but of the humans left behind after the water receded in the Mississippi Valley. Ideas began changing, the most harmful of which was that a deity, or deities, somehow controlled natural forces. Stories were fashioned, feeding off the fear of the survivors for their own safety, and then—just as you see today—power was handed to only a few to steer the course of their history. It was during this time that the idea of mound building was conceived, though it took thousands of years and a much greater population to see it through. Of course, it was obvious that god or gods had nothing to do with any of it, and that it was all about human greed and power." Seesterfekt stares off into the nighttime woods, lost in memory.

"What about the humans from the Hudson Valley flood? What was their reaction to the devastation there?"

"An earlier flood and *its* result was still part of their culture. About twelve hundred years earlier, another glacial lake, Albany your geologists call it, breached its moraine north of what you call the Hudson Highlands. As devastating as it was south of the breached moraine, the flood opened new lowlands with streams and rivers, and created bluffs and hill country on both sides of a one-hundred-eighty-kilometer length of former lake, north of the moraine. The stories and culture of subsequent generations who thrived there went on to shape the ideology of that valley—an ideology devoid of deities, that survives to this day, respecting all life, legged, or winged."

“Speaking of wings,” I say, unable to contain myself any longer. “Do you know Seestergohd Tsitsyoos has wings?!”

"You mean those?" Seest says, pointing toward Jupiter sinking in the southwest, now barely visible through the forest.

Chapter 15

Out of the Darkness

May 15, 2018
New Moon

Fifth Day Moon
continued...

"Is this not great?!" a familiar feminine voice says.

A small body glides into view and lands in my lap. Its lustrous black plumage glistens in the dim first light of dawn. With a provocative gaze, Seestergohd Tsitsyoos leans into my chest, then caresses my face with a wingtip.

"And you, my Teacher," Tsitsyoos says, flitting over and enveloping Seesterfekt with a winged embrace. "You were right."

I jump to my feet with the urgency of a scrambling fighter pilot. "Sorry to break up the party, you two, but I have a few questions!"

Seesterfekt and Tsitsyoos fall to the ground, flailing with laughter. I can't distinguish one from the other.

Looks like a thrashing feather duster.

“Feather duster?” Tsitsyoos says, sitting upright, preparing for my questions.

“Ok, now,” I say, looking at Seesterfekt. “How did you know I was coming here?”

“I told you,” Seest says, sitting up, looking into my eyes. “Tsitsyoos.”

“But how did *you* know?” I ask Tsits.

“I invited you to come here. It was your choice.”

“Did you know,” I say, turning toward Seesterfekt, “that she—Seestergohd Tsitsyoos—well, she was still a she when she was Koodj before—UGH!!—Tsitsyoos had a conversation with me in my head the night of the....”

“Molt?” Tsits says.

“Molt?! I was looking for something more descriptive of what *really* happened that night. But aside from that, I thought humans were unaffected by the domain of impelment.”

“You are,” Seesterfekt says.

“So how do you explain that conversation in my head and the idea that I was invited to come here?”

“These are two different things,” Seest says.

“It was you that night,” Tsitsyoos says. “Not me. Without realizing it, you developed a sense of the Peepl. Over the centuries there *have been* humans open to our consciously unblocked thoughts.”

I look hard at Seesterfekt. "I've never picked up your thoughts."

"No, you haven't," Seest says. "Because I've blocked you. There was no reason, no situation when it was necessary for such contact."

"On Gros Piton," Tsitsyoos says. "Your life *and* my life depended on our sensory connection. I wasn't blocking you, but it was *you* who opened yourself to it."

"But you said—sorry, *conveyed*—that you had been working on the domain of impelment affecting humans."

"I was focused on keeping you alive, not the accuracy of my explanation of why you were hearing me in your head. My answer kept our sensory conversation going, keeping you focused and still. That was more important. My kitties protect me from anything that moves—"

"So really, if I had—"

"Yes."

I need to sit down.

"Teacher said it would happen and it did. Seesterfekt would not have put you in danger."

"But if I had moved?"

"Then you would have put yourself in danger," Seesterfekt says, pointing at me with the two middle fingers of the right hand.

I turn toward Tsitsyoos. "What about being invited here tonight? How is that possible?"

"I was trying to contact you since that morning I jumped from the cliff," Tsits says. "But you are young yet and distance is a problem, though it is improving. Hearing me yesterday morning without being near is proof. Teacher said it would happen and it did."

The distant, fluty notes of a hermit thrush herald the glowing dawn, clearing my mind of confusion. "So that's what you thanked Seesterfekt for? I thought it had something to do with the wings."

"Oh that," Seesterfekt says, shrugging.

"But it's huge, isn't it? I mean it's wings, flying!" I flap my hands.

Tsitsyoos laughs. "It is great to have wings, but remember we hold to the notion that everything changes."

"But it's never happened before, right?" I instantly realize I have no idea if it has or hasn't. "Ok, well one thing I'm pretty sure of is, once Peepl lose their gender, that's it, right? Right?" I push, impatient for confirmation, waiting to spring like a courtroom prosecutor.

Both Seests nod.

I jump to my feet again, focusing my eyes on Tsitsyoos. "So how do you explain that provocative gaze you gave me when you arrived? And what about how you pushed your body against mine, same as the night you molted, *before* losing your gender? And what about that wingtip caress? And that feminine voice at the cliff before you jumped, *after* you molted? Isn't it the same voice you had tonight as you approa—"

"Wait!" Seesterfekt snaps. "Let me guess."

They both giggle.

"Your next words will be, 'Don't wait for the translation! Answer the question!'"

Shit, I WAS recalling that movie scene.

"Do not be ridiculous," Tsitsyoos says. "I was excited. You were too. But always there is a connection to gender when humans get excited. You should practice understanding that a little better. My 'provocative gaze' as you call it, is a trick your gender-bent mind plays on you. We do not feel sexual emotions like you. My emotion for you does not have a word in any of your languages."

The release of tension across my shoulders sends my head forward. Looking at the ground I remember the sting as a first-grade student when realizing my seventh-grade crush wasn't interested in me. I stare off playfully toward the brightening eastern horizon.

We all smile.

Tsitsyoos' last word sticks in my head. I turn my attention to Seesterfekt. "Speaking of languages, aside from you telling me your name in the Peepl language last autumn when we met, you've never said anything else about it."

"It's difficult for humans to follow," Seesterfekt says. "Do you even remember what I told you?"

"Sifōtesuy Yiyōzexulakez Vōxihōzey. O's are always long and emphasized, the other vowels short."

"You gave him the neutral form?" Tsitsyoos says.

"Yes, well, I didn't think he'd remember," Seesterfekt says. "Who remembers these things? Humans never remember these things."

"Neutral form? Humans never remember? What other forms are there?"

"This is not the time or place to begin exploring our language," Tsitsyoos says. "If you would like to know more, Teacher will tell you more. But not now."

I glare at Seesterfekt. "What OTHER forms are there?"

"Ok young fellow, because you remembered what I told you only once, eight lunations ago, I'll give you my name in the female gender, which is one out of four genders and four pre-genders, the neutral form being nongendered."

Maybe I shouldn't have pressed.

"Wūwaxovejinox Sevūfaxow. U's are always long and emphasized, the other vowels short."

"That's not even close to the what you told me last time. And I thought you said O's are always long and emphasized?"

"Yes, in the neutral form. But this is the female gender form."

"Right, well, so," I say, overcome with déjà vu.

"Those are the same three words you mumbled last time I spoke in the Peepl language, which is why I'm surprised you remembered what I said."

"As am I, especially since I can't even remember what we were talking about a few minutes ago."

Tsitsyoos gives a gentle flap.

Right... wings.

"Yes," Seesterfekt says. "There have been what your science calls substitute mutations in our DNA before. What's happened to young Seestergohd Tsitsyoos is a result of at least one of Tsits' Koodjdook living among Tsitsyoos' name-sound bird, the Saint Lucia black finch..." Seesterfekt gazes into the dark woods. "And of course the timing."

Hmm, something evasive about that.

"Tssy-Tssy-Tsits-yoo," a high-pitched bird whistle descending on the fourth syllable emanates from Tsitsyoos. "It was the first sound I heard as a sentient bulb. I chose the last two syllables as my name," Tsits says, shrugging with wingtips up.

Fascinating... Seesterfekt never said anything about the name Purbit. "What's your name-sound bird?"

"I don't have a name-sound bird," Seest says. "Just a sound."

Tsitsyoos quietly giggles.

"Just a sound? Of what?"

"It's not important," Seesterfekt snaps, glaring at Tsitsyoos for what seems an eternity. "It was the first thing I heard." Seest looks at me and gives me the same shoulder shrug as Tsitsyoos did a moment ago.

"Some humans were gathering a certain plant to help with indigestion," Tsitsyoos says. "What was it called?"

"I don't remember what the humans called it then," Seesterfekt says, still looking at me. "You know it as wintergreen."

"Yes, well, these humans were sitting around above Teacher's bulb when the effect of consuming too much tea from the leaves of this plant took hold."

"They farted?" I grin.

"Burped," Seesterfekt says.

"Threw up," Tsitsyoos says.

"More like a wet burp," Seesterfekt insists.

"A biofunction noise," I say. "Purbit is a biofunction noise. Really?"

"Purbit is my name," Seesterfekt says, standing tall.

All our eyes shift back and forth, silently daring each other to laugh first. We smile, spurt, and giggle, finally exploding in raucous guffaws that echo through the forest in the brightening light of dawn.

Watching the sun rise, Seesterfekt, Tsitsyoos, and I greet the day together in silence.

Chapter 16

A More Serious Story

May 15, 2018
New Moon

Fifth Day Moon
continued…

Seesterfekt turns toward Tsitsyoos. "Do you remember what I told you?"

"Yes, I do. Would you like me to tell the story?"

Both of them clear away leaves from the ground and sit, waiting for me.

"I'll begin," Seesterfekt says, nodding. "You ready, my friend?"

Yes, yes, sorry. Tsits just explained the custom.

I clear away some leaves and sit facing them. The damp ground immediately soaks through my pants.

"There was growing unrest among the humans of a particular area because of dwindling resources," Seesterfekt says. "At least that was what their leaders told them. During this time, a new Seestergohd in that area, one who molted with the first pair of wings in thirteen hundred thousand lunations, befriended a human who seemed sincere and honest, but who misunderstood this Seestergohd's vanishing and reappearing as dying and being reborn. Believing the young Seest to be immortal and omnipotent, this human hoped the Seestergohd would stop something terrible that was taking place at the time. He told so many humans what he believed about the Seestergohd, in such a convincing manner, that it caused a collective psychosis among those who were desperate for the hope that something could change their current situation. But this Seestergohd was captured by the leaders of the humans and placed in a cage of woven vines. In trying to escape, the young Seest would vanish, hoping one of the humans would eventually open the cage, but it never happened."

"Why didn't the young Seest stay invisible?"

"At first," Seesterfekt says, nodding at Tsitsyoos. "The young Seestegohd would stay invisible for days."

"But the humans were clever," Tsitsyoos says. "After several efforts by the young Seest, vanishing before their eyes for days, the keepers of this Seest, who the humans called Gohd—"

"Stop!" I say. "You're telling me the name God came from Seestergohd?"

"No, I was not telling you that. Were you not listening?"

"Yes, I was, but—"

"He does this sometimes," Seesterfekt says.

"The leaders of the humans," Tsitsyoos continues, glaring at me, "abbreviated Seestergohd to Gohd because of an ancient legend of a small vanishing deity named Goad, who lived before mankind existed."

"Any connection to that?" I ask Seesterfekt, suspecting the Peepl were at the center of this legend.

"No." Purbits laughs. "That deity breathed fire and lived in a volcano."

"Oh."

"And ate humans," Tsitsyoos says. "Before they could be born. That is why it existed before mankind. Until one human, according to legend, tricked it and escaped out of the Gohd's volcano when it erupted. The human landed in a swamp, where it cooled off enough to be born, then multiplied and spread across the world."

"Wonderful story. But what's this got to do with the winged Seestergohd?"

"Nothing," Tsits says. "You interrupted that story."

"But I was simply trying to... You know what? Forget it."

"As I was saying before," Tsits says. "After several efforts by the young Seest, vanishing before their eyes for days, the keepers of this Gohd made thin golden rods, gently crisscrossing them through the cage, causing the captive young Seest to reappear."

Fascinating.

"Touching a vanished Seest with anything conductive," Seesterfekt says, "disrupts the electrical balance needed to sustain the negative refraction of light rays. *Shorting out* is a simpler way of putting it."

"Why haven't you mentioned the young Seestergohd's name, or the name of the place, or what the humans called themselves, or a timeline other than 'wings hadn't happened in thirteen-hundred-thousand moons?"

"Lunations," Seest says.

"Yes, fine, *lunations*. But you named Ankit-ip and Ptk of your Faabl years. You told me about what humans were doing then, and the reasons for what they were doing. Why not with this story?"

"It's as I mentioned before," Seest says. "Everything I tell you is true. Some accounts, like those of Ptk and Ankit-ip can never be substantiated with evidence. But with these accounts my friend, as in the stories of the mastodons, there *is* the evidence your science seeks, if you're willing to look outside the box. These things we tell you now have been uncovered by humans—all evidence of it is in front of you. But your propensity to create a past reality in the image of your present preconception blinds you."

"So why tell me? Why tell me anything about the past?"

"That is enough for me," Tsitsyoos says, flying up and vanishing into the sparse deciduous canopy.

“Me too,” Seesterfekt says, vanishing while descending the steep south slope of our mini piton gathering place.

“Right,” I call out. “Not rude. Just your way. Nice talkin’ to ya, always a pleasure. I’ll just sit here. Don’t worry about me.”

As spring inches toward summer, deciduous trees, fully open in the valleys, unfurl toward leaf-out at summits. Grass needs mowing, weeds need whacking, wood needs splitting—all healthy diversions from the alternate reality I'm a part of in which little hair-feathered Peepl roam—and fly—around.

I can't tell from one minute to the next whether I'm simply thinking of Seesterfekt and Tsitsyoos or they're trying to contact me, but the urge to sleep out along the river tonight is too strong to resist. I'm heading for the woods, forsaking my chores.

Chapter 17

Gifted

May 29, 2018
Full Moon

Sixth Whole Moon

While gathering wood for the night's fire, I recall familiar scenes from downriver—dodging splash and spray just inches above the water, weaving in and out of riverbank trees, soaring high above the ravine—

Wait... these aren't my memories... this is in real time... Seestergohd Tsitsyoos?... it's Tsits flying up the valley...

Apparently, this was an invitation.

Wow, this is new.

"It certainly is," Tsitsyoos says, landing on the pile of sticks I've gathered. "I was not consciously blocking you on the way here, but I also was not trying to communicate with you," Tsits says with a big chicklet grin. "You read me, in real time, on your own."

"What does it mean?" I ask, excited yet apprehensive.

"Hmm... Maybe I should let Seesterfekt explain."

"It's about the molt, isn't it?"

Tsitsyoos eyes flash white.

That's new too... "You're surprised, aren't you?"

"Surprised?" Tsits eyes flash white again.

"I'm guessing, but I'd say white eyes are a reaction to surprise that you can't control any more than Seesterfekt can control the iridescent green-eyed reaction to seeing a bottle of Chimay red."

Tsits eyes flash white several times.

"And the fact that you're surprised at my question tells me you're unable to read my mind right now because I don't want you to. Is that true?"

"Yes."

"You know, I started questioning what was going on the night of your molt, when you explained how the Peepl names have suffixes to indicate gender. It didn't escape my notice that my guide was female and the Koodj she protected was Koodj Khetchishsht, a male. Curious thing you being female and me being male also, don't you think?"

"Not curious," Tsits says, motioning with a wingtip, then walking toward sitting stones at the fire pit. "Deliberate. Koodj Khetchishsht and I were the last hope for Lucian Peepl." Tsitsyoos gives a quick wing flap, then sits. "We grew up together on the island and thought the molt would happen to us at the same time. We realized at first position of the solar year—December twenty-first, 2009, by your reckoning—that Khetchishsht would molt earlier than I, sometime in late June of your 2010. Teacher visited the island during first lunation of that year and met with a woman willing to stay with Koodj Khetchishsht the night of his molt. That woman was your guide. She has been my friend from birth."

"From birth? Come on, how is that possible?"

"She is a true human being."

"What does that mean, exactly?"

"It's a rather long explanation for another time perhaps."

Great... "Where is Khetchishsht now?"

"Gone, only young Seestergohd Khetchishsht's dark energy remains."

"I'm sorry. What happened?"

"Khetch flew into a plane and was killed."

"What? How? Why didn't Khetchishsht's sensory domain detect the dark energy of all the humans inside?"

"Oh, it did. Khetch was... playing."

You're kidding...

"No, it happened on the island you call Trinidad, in your year 2010, on July fourteenth, two days past seventh day moon. Half a lunation after Khetchishsht's molt."

I'm sorry. I feel your sadness.

"I know you do. Thank you. But there's more than sadness to this story."

"Continue, please."

"American Airlines flight 1668 was scheduled for your city of Miami. It was a Boeing company, 767-300. After Ketch struck it during takeoff, the plane returned to Piarco International Airport in Trinidad."

"Was anyone hurt?" *SHIT!* I instantly realize my insensitivity.

"No," Tsits says with all the sarcasm I braced for. "Just some stupid bird was killed."

"I'm so sorry. Really. I am."

"I understand. You cannot help it. It is all that *sapiens*-centric upbringing. It was reported that none of the two hundred twelve humans aboard were injured. But the birdlike creature retrieved from the aircraft was not reported. This news will never get out. Khetchishsht's body became the property of Boeing, which happily shared it with your government in an agreement that Boeing engineers be part of the team that analyzed the creature. The company also received all rights to any technologies deemed valuable for government contract, or releasable for consumer use in recognition of its cooperation."

Do I need to know all this?

"You asked me to continue after I said there was more than sadness to this story. Besides, it will help your understanding as more things become known to you."

"Speaking of things becoming known, I thought we were sitting down here so you could tell me what's happening to me?"

"Patience," Tsits says. "Few humans receive this. You and the woman who was with Koodj Khetchishsht are the first since the capture of the Seestergohd that Teacher and I told you about."

"It was Wookwahs," a voice calls, emerging from the forest.

"Teacher!"

"Wookwahs came through our molt with wings," Seesterfekt says, nodding a greeting to us both. "And it was I who made friends with the human, not Seestergohd Wookwahs."

My eyebrows squinch. "What are you saying?"

"It was *my* human friend, Eyingamyus, that told others about Wookwahs, mistakenly believing he was chosen as a go-between of the Gohds since being transformed by exposure to our molt."

"Wait-wait-wait. Back up a bit. How was a yingamiss exposed to your molt?"

"Eyingamyus," Tsitsyoos says, giggling.

"Yes, that. If there were two of the Peepl present, why was this Eyingamyus there?"

"He found Wookwahs and I molting," Seesterfekt says. "All our strength was on that, and maintaining our domains. We weren't pleased Eyingamyus found us, especially since he arrived with the repugnant misconception of being chosen to be present at such a *miraculous moment*, as he called it. But there was nothing we could do. Remember, humans aren't affected by the domain of impelment."

"But Khetchishsht also had wings," I say, probing for clarity while preparing a tinder bundle for the evening fire.

"Before Khetchishsht passed through the molt with wings, one hundred thirty thousand lunations after Wookwahs," Tsitsyoos says, "and I passed through the molt with wings ninety-seven lunations after Ketch, it was as Seesterfekt told you, last day moon: thirteen hundred thousand lunations."

"And before that?" I ask Seesterfekt.

"Thirteen hundred thousand."

"So that's been a thing, a constant. Every 1.3 million moons—sorry, lunations. Roughly 100,000 years," I say, striking sparks from a ferro rod onto dry tinder.

"It was," Tsitsyoos says. "Until Ketch, and myself."

"Three winged Peepl, three altered humans. Did this ever happen before your time?"

"No," Seest says.

I feed the kindled flame a few sticks of wood.

"It's a result of my early contact with humans. Breaking The Forbidden allowed all this to happen."

"So you just took it upon yourself to change hundreds of thousands of years of wisdom to create a few altered humans."

"This is unproductive reasoning," Tsits snaps.

"It's millions of years," Seesterfekt says, laughing and shrugging. "But who's counting?"

"You are blaming Teacher for altering humans, but the truth is, these changes in you are a result of exposure to something in your environment, something that has always been here. For millions of years, we watched, wandering alone, as humans evolved. The Forbidden was in place to protect us both. But we are dying and so are you."

"What do you mean we're dying?!"

"Let me, young Seestergohd," Seesterfekt says, raising an arm.

Tsitsyoos' wings flutter and slap the air as young Seestergohd turns and walks away.

"We are dying, it's true. We will pass. There is only one bulb left and one Koodj. The rest of us are Seest, Manthasif, and Satcher. We accept this. You, however, don't address your reality. This planet's biosphere can't sustain itself under the stress you're exerting on it. Your population is too high and it grows every day. Your civilizations and the industrial and technological revolutions, as you call them, are alien entities—artificial ideas brought to bear on a natural world. You humans truly don't see the end result of your presence here. This all began after the last glacial maximum. It always begins after the melting of ice. But this time, you've spread across the globe in a geologic blink of an eye, instituting government systems inadequate for the task. Socialist republics, dictatorships, monarchies, theocracies, democracies, communist states—all designed to keep humanity from unraveling for the benefit of the wealthiest. Your politics makes pawns of you all. You look to the heavens for salvation. First it was in the form of your deities, and now it's through your science. The salvation you hope for exists: other planets, ripe for the taking, like the New World of the Europeans. But what will you do to these worlds if you make it there? Do you think you'll behave any differently? Do you think your science will save you? Do you think one planet's history won't repeat on another? What you call altered is what we the Peepl have been for tens of millions of years. To reach out and know the thoughts of other beings is to understand your place in the Universe in a way humanity can't conceive. Even now, as I speak of it, your thoughts turn only to the dangers of knowing other's thoughts, not to empathy."

Seesterfekt breathes deep, then nods at Tsitsyoos, now walking back toward us.

"What Teacher is saying is that we are passing," Tsitsyoos says. "This is not changeable. But your condition as humans is. Your fate on this planet is not sealed, yet. But to survive you will need to evolve beyond your human limitation for understanding. And you verify this limitation by calling *altered* what we call *gifted*."

All I've done for the last two weeks is wander the forest trying to digest the idea of being gifted. *Hm, wandering alone... am I a Watcher Wandering Alone?*

Chapter 18

A Reunion

June 13, 2018
New Moon

Sixth Day Moon

"Not quite." Seestergohd Tsitsyoos giggles, gliding in from the east on slight wing beats, and landing in a nearby beech tree. "Did Teacher show you where we are meeting?"

"Yes."

"Do you know the place?"

"It's a high meadow, tucked away on a hillside facing east. I've seen it from a distance before, but I've never been there and don't know the best way."

"So where are you walking to?"

"Tsits, I've been wandering every day since our last meeting at the river, but I don't know why. I'm not crazy, yet. But I feel different. And the thoughts I've been having are thoughts I've never had before."

"Poor you." Tsitsyoos laughs.

"Really? You think this is funny? What if you suddenly had a huge change in who you—"

"Poor you," Tsits says, stretching both wings then slapping them back in place. "Stop wallowing. I will fly ahead and show you the way. Try to pay attention so you do not wander off. It will be the first time a human has ever witnessed this. And it is all the more important because it will be the last time it will ever happen."

Why do I feel a sudden wave of deep sadness?

"Because you are of the Peepl now," Tsitsyoos says, jumping from the beech limb and flying north.

. . .

As I approach Seesterfekt and Tsitsyoos sitting on a blowdown overlooking the meadow, they appear as twins, motionless. I sense their silent conversation. They're worried about me.

"Sorry to interrupt."

"You're not interrupting young fellow. We're both very glad you're here," Seesterfekt says, moving over so I can sit between them.

Tsitsyoos gazes at me with an oversized toothy grin.

Is it the teeth, or am I over the gender-biased emotions?

"It is the teeth," Tsits says, grinning grander. "I did it on purpose."

Tall grass and sedge dominate the meadow. Bloomless aster and half-height Joe Pie thicken the lower end, where brambles, scattered throughout, shade spruce and fir saplings. A tree frog's bleat and thrush's flute undulate over the meadow in the early evening chill.

"How are you my friend?" Seesterfekt says, looking over the meadow.

"Adjusting. Well, trying."

"Good, good, and your questions?"

How do I explain... it would take forever...

"We have time," Tsitsyoos says. "The lightening bugs are still sleeping."

"How is this possible? I mean— How did I—"

"I know what you mean," Seesterfekt says, nodding. "During molt, strands of DNA release into the surrounding air. If they're breathed in and bind to the lining of human sinuses of the opposite gender, they have a chance of growing deep into the brain. Seeking out and lodging in what your science calls the corpus callosum, these DNA strands assist that organ in utilizing and coordinating the various lobes. But these strands do more than boost the corpus callosum's performance or amplify its effect. The human brain, in effect, hybridizes."

"With four genders and four pre-genders of the Peepl, and the myriad gender distinctions of humans, how can you speak simply of *opposite* genders?"

"Remember, we're not bound by your social constructs. The Peepl don't put weight on gender distinction beyond identifiers. There are certain unfolding expectations—such as opposite gender Koodjdook produce a bulb, and same-gender molting does not—but since everything changes, it doesn't matter to us in the way it does to you. We've lost the possession of permanent gender, so who cares?" Seest laughs.

"What Teacher is trying to say," Tsitsyoos says, "is that when referring to the molt, we the Peepl assume gender as a sexual designator: female or male."

"That's what you were trying to say?"

"Yes, well, I was getting there," Seesterfekt says.

"So why does it have to be the opposite gender?"

"Why does what have to be the opposite gender?" Seest says, visibly perplexed.

"Purbits! Come on. Between the Peepl and humans."

"Ah—"

"We do not know," Tsits says, understanding my frustration.

"We only know that it occurs," Seesterfekt says, catching up to the conversation. "The other peculiarity is that it occurs only when the Peepl come out of the molt with wings."

I stare at Tsitsyoos. "So your DNA is now inside my brain, enhancing its function?"

"Yes, and over time, hybridizing it. We are in effect, according to your science, sister and brother, sharing some of the same DNA."

"So that's how my guide was able to know what I was thinking. She breathed in Koodj Khetchishsht's male DNA during his molt and was gifted the same way."

"Yes, and she is a good woman, a true human being," Seesterfekt says. "She lost Ketch shortly after the molt, but hasn't lost heart, even now."

"Non, mwen pa te! No, I hahv note!"

My jaw drops. My eyes scan the wooded edge of the meadow.

"Why yoa broad me heah to dis coowl foarest? If I yahm goin' walkin' in di foarest, let it be in di wahm Looshian jungahl." My former guide emerges from the woods, wagging her finger. "Doan be lookin' hoppy to see me! Ahnd doan be ahskin' no names neadah," she says, staring at me with wide open eyes.

"Koodjuman!" Tsitsyoos says, leaping from our communal log.

"Koodjuman?" I ask Seesterfekt.

"Yes, well, that's what young Koodj Tsitsyoos used to call her. It's a playful, familial blending of terms."

"You hid it from me, all of you," Tsitsyoos says, hovering alongside Koodjuman as she walks the woods edge toward us.

"Don't look at me sister," I say. "I had no idea either."

"Yehs," Koodjuman says, winking at Seesterfekt. "We keep ah good secreht well. Ahnd how iz my FayKoodJee?"

"FayKoodJee?" I ask Seesterfekt, as I stand to greet her.

Seesterfekt grins, then nods with eyes closed.

"So dare. My name to yoa iz Koodjuman." She laughs, hugging me. "Di lass time I saw yoa— Oh! Wotah mess yoa waz! Ahnd yoa, Ole Pawbit," she says, kneeling down, embracing Seesterfekt in both hands. "Tank yoa foah callin' me heah ahnd ahgreein' to di suhprize foah FayKoodJee. I waz sahd when yoa left," she says, looking at Tsits, now comfortably nestled against her chest. "But I knewit waz note foahevah."

"No, it was not forever. After tonight, we will go home together."

"Ah yehs, ah big night it iz!"

Seesterfekt motions to Koodjuman and moves over, giving her room on the log next to me. A gentle breeze greets twilight in the east.

"Poukisa ou santi konsa?" Koodjuman turns toward me. Her words knock Seesterfekt and Tsitsyoos off the log, laughing.

"Why do you smell so bad?" Seesterfekt says between guffaws.

Great... they all know Lucian—

"Wait, doan tell me! Yoa hahv bin wandahrin'."

"Yes, exactly!"

"And dare iz no watah weahr yoa wandah?"

Seesterfekt and Tsitsyoos laugh so hard, they gasp for air, grasping their abdomens.

Koodjuman laughs with them. "Tande non, nou tou le de, li gen non deja?" she says.

Seesterfekt sits up, covered in dirt. "Well, no, he doesn't."

"No he doesn't what?" I say.

Tsitsyoos stands up, flapping wings, flinging dirt everywhere. "Koodjuman asked if you have a name yet."

"Bon petèt nou ta dwe rele l, DedjoTah, " Koodjuman says, laughing.

Seesterfekt and Tsitsyoos grab their abdomens again, shriek and fall to the ground, writhing in laughter. Dirt flings past me. I walk away, shaking my head, leaving the three of them to recover while I wander some distance into the woods to pee.

I return to my companions, who now sit in silence, and we four watch darkness descend on the meadow.

Chapter 19
A Missing Piece

June 13, 2018
New Moon

Sixth Day Moon
continued...

"What's a DedjoTah?" I whisper to Koodjuman, assuming it was the name she proposed for me.

She smiles. "Iz wohn ov dare ole words—ainchahnt word dat mean sōmdin' like, 'its muddah needs to wash it.'"

"I know dis new ding goinon in yoar head," she says, searching my eyes. "But yoa'll get yoostoo it, ahnd it will mek yoa ah beddah pahson. Do note be afray of di tawts it evohkes. Di Peepl DNA ahz no violent tendahncy ahnd cawz no violent re-ahkshon. Di ideah ov powah from dis fades in ah lunāshiohn. Yoa doan hahv to wohry. Doan fear yoar tawts righ now. Juss ledthem pahss ahnd yoa'll be ah beddah pahson."

I nod. "Thank you."

"You have questions DedjoTah?" Seesterfekt says.

"Yes, first, can you not call me that?" I say, smiling.

"Of course."

"Thank you. Now, I'm curious about Saint Lucia—the connection to the Peepl—how and when did they arrive there?"

"We have time," Seest says, nodding to Tsitsyoos and Koodjuman.

"The first of the Peepl to visit what humans now call Saint Lucia," Tsitsyoos says, "was a winged Seestergohd from somewhere north whose name is forgotten. It was during your early Pliocene epoch, almost four million years ago. The Pitons as you know them didn't exist at that time, but the northern part of the island was lush beyond your imagination—a primeval forest where insect, frog, and bird song filled the air."

"Uhndreds ov tousahnds ov yeahs pahss befoah ahnudda winged Seestahgohd come to di Island," Koodjuman says. "Dat wonz name iz ahlso lost. Many cōmin' to di island ovah milliohns ov yeahs, wyle di fah nort freeze ahn tawd, aghen ahn aghen. Awl dees cōmin' froam di nort. Awl dare names hahv bin foahgotton."

"Seestergohd Zoobzoots was the first of the Peepl remembered as being in Saint Lucia," Tsitsyoos says. "Zoobzoots flew up from the South American mainland about one hundred and ten thousand years ago during the late Pleistocene epoch, and settled near the Soufriere volcanic complex: my home.

“So,” I say, looking at Seesterfekt, “Seestergohd Zoobzoots was the last winged Peepl before your molting partner, Seestergohd Wookwahs. Yes?”

“You’re paying attention my friend.” Seest nods.

“Zoobzoots waz di firss Peepl travahlin’ froam Ahfrica to Sout AhmerIca wit di firss humahns dat ahlso ahrive froam di east.”

“WHAT?”

“That’s his favorite word,” Seesterfekt says, smiling.

“Yehs… In doze days, when di ohshiohns weah low becawz ov di ice in di fah nort ahnd sout, di distahnce bahtween di outah islands of Sout Ahmerica ahnd doze ov Ahfrica waz less dan two tousand kilomeetahs. Ehvy woodahn boats cōmin’ cross di Ahtlahntic Ohshiohn in less dan ah lunāshiohn, ahnd sōmtime fahstah yoozin’ smahl saylz, med ov tick elephahnt hide. Dare iz ahn ole tayle dat say ah Spahnish preese tawt di Caribs aboud saylz.” Koodjuman laughs. “But di Ahfricahns waz yoozin’ di saylz wyle Spen waz ah baddellgroun’ bahtween yoar Neahndahtal ahnd Heidlbahgensas.” She laughs even harder. “Di Black Caribs ahr note descend froam slaves, no! Dat waz good propagahnda foah di white Europēahn coloniss. But evrybohdy knowit dat di Ahfricahns ahrive in AhmerIca ah lōng tyme befoah di Europēahns name it dat.”

“Everybody?” I say, bewildered. “I didn’t know.”

“Yehs well, yoa ahr nobohdy.” Koodjuman laughs again.

"But what about Saint Lucia?" I ask again.

"The island was inhabited by descendants of humans who had earlier migrated by land from Asia into North and South America," Tsitsyoos says. "The islands in the Caribbean were easy to reach during glacial maximum, when sea levels were low. Few humans liked making the journey, but enough explored and settled all the islands that were big enough to support at least a few family groups. After establishing themselves in what is now known as Brazil, the African descendants of early voyagers across the Atlantic also made their way west and north through Central America and north along the Caribbean island chain. For tens of thousands of years, all along the Great Circle, humans traded and mixed among each other as humans do."

"The Great Circle?" I say.

"Awl di lahnd dat suhroundin' di Caribbēahn Sea. Awl di humahns waz gettin' alawn till di wohnz in di Yookahtahn Peninsahla change."

"It was a similar change," Seesterfekt says, "that I told you about with *Homo heidelbergensis."* Humans in the Yucatán Peninsula began sacrificing others to appease the forces that kept the Universe turning. They had knowledge of things you still don't, and no one knows how they got it. It was knowledge of things that didn't make sense to them, things beyond their comprehension. They feared and condemned it, and focused their fear outward. It happened overnight. One day, relative peace. The next day, violence exploded and spread throughout the Great Circle. All the humans within the circle feared them."

"Dees Ohlmec Yookahtahns hahd note mix wit di Ahfricahns. Di Ohlmecs hahd begun ceremoniahl humahn sahcrifice to di Univahs az ahn introduckshiahn to a much lahdjah plahn. Di leadahs decidehd to erahdicate Ahfricahns froam di Great Sirkehl, sayin' dat day did note belong dare, eevahn dough day hahd settle on di islahnds tens ov tousahnds ov yeahs earliah. Doze leadahs hahd bin holdin' bach food resahves to show dat wot day cahn produce waz down becawz di clīmaht waz changin'—di weddah waz dryah. But dare waz still two lahdj hahvest of maize, bean, squash ahn othah crops, twice a yeah."

"Olmec populations were easily convinced that the Universe demanded a sacrificial outpouring, and that the Africans were it," Seesterfekt says. "Olmec raiding parties traveled great distances to capture any Africans to sacrifice them. Once the frenzy took hold, it wasn't difficult to include mixed bloods, since the purebloods already sacrificed hadn't appeased the Universe enough to change the climate."

"The friend of Old Purbits who was of natural lineage," Tsitsyoos says, "thought he was chosen to stop the slaughter because of his ability to read the leader's minds."

"Eyingamyus?"

"Yes. He discovered the plot devised by the pureblood group to rid themselves of who they did not want, claiming it was the will of the Universe. So he spread the news of these Gohds who could die and be reborn, and spoke of one that could even fly. He told whoever would listen that the Africans, after all these thousands of years, still respected and honored these Gohds. Many non-African humans began showing an interest in what Eyingamyus had to say. One day he and a group of followers were brought before the leaders in full view of the population to make and support their claim."

"Tinkahn he hahd di mōmnt he'd bin waitin' foah, dis young mahn describe di blahk fehdah Gohds ahnd how di Ahfricahns hahd kept as pahrt ov dare coolchyah, di remembrahnce ov Seestahgohd Zoobzoots. Dey ohnored dat memohry ahnd tayles ov dings dare ancestahs learn froam di Peepl, who waz livin' in di Great Sirkehl ahlso. He describe wot day cahn do, ahnd di powah day givin' him to read di mines. He tell how he cahn read di leadah's mines ahnd reveahl di whole plot."

"There was a great silence among the crowd," Tsitsyoos says, "until a cage with Seestergohd Wookwahs in it was displayed for all to see. There were golden rods crisscrossing the cage. When removed, the small, black-feathered Gohd, now ridiculed as the false Gohd of Africans, would vanish to the amazement of the crowd. Inserting the gold rods again made the black-feathered false Gohd reappear. Repeatedly doing this brought insults from the crowd and discredited the young man and his followers. They were sacrificed on the spot, and the slaughter continued with renewed vigor. Fortunately for Wookwahs, the purebloods *did* fear this Gohd, so killing it was deemed dangerous, though keeping it captive was now key to maintaining the fervor."

"The famous stone heads," Seesterfekt says, "at La Venta, San Lorenzo, Tres Zapotes, and La Cobata along the coast north of the Yucatán Peninsula, all depict African or mixed African facial features. The placement of these stone heads indicated the northern boundary line of where those humans were at that time, and, more ominously, they served as wanted posters. No one with those features was safe there. It was a huge success in keeping African descendants contained within the Great Circle. None could pass that area and not be noticed and captured."

"Weren't the Olmec of African descent?" I ask, having read a little about them.

"There are theories among humans that the Olmec may have had African origins," Tsitsyoos says. "But that is not true. The Olmec were of Asian descent. They had traveled to and through North America hundreds of thousands of years before the Africans arrived."

"Dātin' ov di stone heads ahnd artifahcts is wrong. Day ahr aboud ten tousahnd yeahs ole."

"It's true," Seesterfekt says. "The Olmec, as you call them, are the ones that captured Wookwahs. Naturally, in their thinking, this deity had to be captured and subdued in the overall effort to rid the Great Circle of African blood."

"This sounds like some sci-fi movie plot," I say, shaking my head, trying to fathom all this happening so long ago.

"Unfortunately," Seest says. "It's not fiction but part of the past, present, and future reality with humans."

"But where does Saint Lucia fit into all this?"

“Pa ka tann, moun sa yo, wi pwofesè granmoun.” Koodjuman laughs. “Cahn’t wait dees humahns, yehs ole Teacha?”

“I took advantage of the arrogance of the moment,” Seesterfekt says, “and freed Wookwahs that night. Wook flew ahead, revealing the safest trails for me to take east toward the coast where African bloods were escaping in boats, following the deep trench south of the Cayman Islands to the Island of Jamaica. Deep water didn’t scare African bloods, but the Olmec feared it. Tales of stars falling from the sky into the deep and then becoming monsters that ate humans in the night kept them close to land. After a short rest in Jamaica, escaping Africans continued east along the southern coasts of what are now Haiti, the Dominican Republic, and Puerto Rico. From there they fanned out south along the island chain. The group we traveled with landed and settled in what became Saint Lucia.”

“Iz tyme Teacha.” Koodjuman points toward the meadow. “Faabahl Peewee iz cōmin' 'round.”

In the dark of this moonless night, lightning bugs' furious courtship illuminates condensing air, setting green haze over the meadow. A synesthetic wonder—tonight, they peak.

Chapter 20

The Last is the First

June 14, 2018
New Moon

A Few Hours past Sixth Day Moon
continued...

Faabl PeeWee?

"Yes," Seesterfekt says. "Faabl has chosen the eastern wood-pewee song as a name.

"Thank goodness it's not the eastern phoebe." *Incessant repetitious song...*

"You don't know about the ovenbirds, do you?"

"Doan be ahskin' him aboud di bawds. He will nehvah stohp!"

"Ovenbirds?" I glare at Koodjuman. "Yes, I know what they are."

"And their song?" Seest says.

"Teacher-teacher-teacher..." I purse my lips and stare at Seest. "Are you kidding me?"

"No, I'm not. Ovenbirds and their close relatives, the northern and Louisiana water thrushes, all sounded very similar till about four hundred eleven years ago when the English settled in Jamestown."

"I like dis story," Koodjuman says, nodding.

"You know, that was a gamble you took, Teacher," Tsitsyoos says.

Can't wait to hear this one...

"Well good, I'll tell you," Seesterfekt says with a grin. "In 1607, when the English settled Jamestown, I spent some time with them—"

"With them?"

"Ok, around them. It was easy to see that of all the humans sailing west across the Atlantic in *those* days, the English, would, after a while, dominate a large area of the North American continent. And that meant English would be the new language. It wasn't very difficult to suggest to ovenbirds that they become the new heralds of emerging Faabl from that point on."

"Is this a joke?"

Koodjuman and Tsitsyoos shake their heads.

Really?

"It's true," Seesterfekt says. "They agreed to build their oven-shaped nests over any of the Peepl bulbs in the ground each spring. A short heralding display as each new Faabl emerges was also part of their agreement."

The sound of *teacher-teacher-teacher, teachyoo, teachyoo* emanates from within the bordering forest.

"Like that," Seest says, pointing across the meadow.

. . .

Here in the woods of Winhall, before the break of dawn, an ovenbird heralds the new teacher as we hold our collective breaths, waiting for the last Faabl in history to walk out of the woods.

. . .

The flutter of wings from the forest edge echoes across the meadow.

Koodjuman peers ahead. "Do yoar ohvenbawd go wit di Faabahl when day emahge?"

"I don't know," Seesterfekt says. "This is the first Faabl to emerge since the ovenbirds agreed—"

"What?! That whole story?" I say. "And all that effort was for one Faabl, that's it?"

Tsitsyoos jumps and hovers next to me. "It is a very important Faabl. I will go to the forest and see what is happening."

"But," I whisper to Seesterfekt. "I hear ovenbirds sing like that several times a day in late spring and early summer, usually at dusk, night, or dawn."

"Ovenbirds never give up hope. That's why I chose them," Seest says, anxiously peering toward the woods edge.

Tsitsyoos returns, mumbling, “The last is the first.”

“FayKoodJee, wot iz wrong?”

“The last is the first,” Tsits repeats.

“What’s Tsits talking about?”

“The last is the first,” Seesterfekt says, staring up into the shadowed limbs of a woods-edge beech. “It’s true. I never saw it coming.”

Shrugging, I turn toward Koodjuman. “Saw what?”

“Dat!” she says, pointing toward the shadow Seesterfekt stares at.

A dark shape, gliding from the tree, lands in my lap as I quell my urge to move. It’s no bigger than a little brown bat.

“I’m Paable Fehweewee,” it says in the tiniest of high-pitched voices.

Makes Alvin the chipmunk sound like a baritone...

“Paable Fehweewee,” it says again, hopping over to Koodjuman. “Fehweewee. Paable Fehweewee,” it repeats.

I giggle with joy, like a toddler taking their first steps.

“I havingz preech bloprems.”

“Speech problems? Yes, you are PeeWee,” I say, apparently the only one able to cope with the unexpected condition of little Faabl.

"Can you vanish?" I ask, reaching into my pocket.

"I non't doe."

"Try." I pull out my truck keys as PeeWee slowly vanishes, pressing them against the slight resistance I feel where our new Faabl was a moment ago.

"Pthank you!" little Faabl says, reappearing.

"How did you know to do that?" Seesterfekt asks.

"Wookwahs," I say, shrugging. "Seestergohd Wookwahs and the golden rods. I thought shorting out little Faabl might reset speech. It was a wild guess."

"Pwhy is everyone staring at me?" PeeWee asks. "And pwhat does *the last is the first* mean?"

"You have wings, PeeWee," Tsitsyoos says, finally able to articulate.

"So do you," little Faabl says, with an oversized chicklet grin.

"Tsitsyoos cōmin' troo di molt wit wings. Darahr no Peepl ehvah hahv emahge wit di wings. Ahnd nehvah wonz who cahn vahnish eadah."

"Pteacher," PeeWee says. "I have pwings, but I don't really know anypthing. Shouldn't I know pthings? Shouldn't I sense pthings? I feel like somepthing is missing."

"Do you sense any of the dark energy around us?" Seesterfekt says.

"Pwhat's dark energy?"

"Oh! We ahr hahvin' ah prōblem wit dis wohn FayKoodJee."

"What did you sense while you were bulb?" I ask.

"No-pthing."

"Did you feel nothing of the world outside your bulb?" Seesterfekt says.

"No-pth."

"So how did you know who we are?" Seest says. "Or to let us know when you were emerging? Or that you chose PeeWee as your name?"

"I non't doe any of you except Pteacher," little PeeWee says, looking back and forth at each of us, then fixing eyes on Seesterfekt. "I non't doe how I know you, or how I contacted you, or how I know my name, or pwhy you all stare at me peecause I have pwings,"

"It's not just the pwing—ugh!—*wings,* PeeWee," I say. "You have the black coat of a Seestergohd after molt, yet you've only just emerged tonight. That coat you wear is three thousand years ahead of any coat any Faabl has ever had." *Oh... shit... what if I'm wrong... again—*

"You're right this time," Seesterfekt says. "This is the first."

"I'm the first Faabl with pwings and a plack coat! Pwhat does it mean? Is it a new peeginning? Are pwee evolving?"

I glare at little Faabl. "How do you know about something as complex as evolution, but not know any of the answers to the questions Seesterfekt Purbits asked you? If you didn't sense anything as bulb, where did you get your understanding?"

"I non't doe," little Faabl says, jumping up and hovering above us.

At the woods edge, now slightly illuminated by the breaking dawn, a white great horned owl appears, racing toward us from the shadows.

I turn to PeeWee. *Where's little Faa—*

An explosion of colliding bodies echoes across the meadow. Flailing wingbeats drop from the sky into the green haze below.

"From the moment Faabl PeeWee appeared... domains were numb," Seesterfekt says. "This what little Faabl feels... Never sensed the owl... You sense anything... Any of you... Anything from PeeWee... Tsits, you... Never mind... Fly over there and see if Faabl is alive... Koodjuman... nothing."

I've never seen Seesterfekt like this... "Easy, Old Purbits. Tsits is on the way."

Chapter 21

A Silent Conversation

June 14, 2018
Waxing Crescent Moon

A Few Hours past Sixth Day Moon
continued...

"Is PeeWee alive?" Seesterfekt yells.

"Give her—I mean Tsits—a minute... Here she—Ugh!"

"Boat ov yoa be calm! FayKoodjee iz cōmin'."

"I do not see or sense little Faabl anywhere," Tsitsyoos says, returning from the meadow where PeeWee and the owl fell to the ground. "Like you Teacher, I have not sensed anything since the moment PeeWee appeared."

"If yoa ahr boat nomb ahnd weah when PeeWee ahrive, den maybe Faabahl PeeWee iz still neah. Maybe Faabahl vahnish ahnd cahn note re-ahpeah. Yoa know, dat new littahl wohn iz very diffrehnt. Teacha, FayKoodjee, go dare towahd doze needahl trees up di hill. We'ahl stay heah. Leht's see wot hoppon den."

Koodjuman and I wait as Seesterfekt and Tsitsyoos head up the hill. “I've been sensing Seesterfekt and Tsitsyoos and you, but I didn't sense Faabl PeeWee at all.”

“I did. Note awl di tyme, note now, but I did.”

“Their domains are sensing everything again.”

“How do yoa knowit?

“It's like a memory. When they convey something through their domains, it's like a memory.”

“Yehs, I know dat. Juss say dey tellin' yoa!”

“They're telling me!”

“Dare!” Koodjuman says, pointing then running across the meadow, waving at me to follow. “Littahl Faabahl iz dare, weah dey fell.”

I'm winded from the sprint over. “Where? I don't see anything.”

“GIMMIE YOAR KEYS!”

Same tone she used the morning after Tsitsyoos' molt.

“Yehs, it iz. I waz wohryd den too. Dees ahr hour Peepl. Yoa should be wohryd ahlso.”

Our Peepl... It took her to say it for me to see it... Our Peepl...

Seesterfekt and Tsitsyoos return to the meadow.

"Hey," I blurt. "Day tellin me day don't sense nutting agan."

Koodjuman spins her head and torso around, pointing her finger like it was a weapon of mass destruction. "Doan be mehkin' fun ov me mistah!"

I laugh.

Kneeling with outstretched arm, keys in hand, Koodjuman gently sweeps the air a few inches above the ground till the keys hit something unseen. As she holds the keys there, PeeWee materializes with a toothy smile covering most of the little Faabl's face.

That's different... looks like a little brown bat with teeth for a head.

"Yoa skayah us awl, yoa know dat, littahl FayPooBee." Koodjuman picks up PeeWee in her cupped hands.

Why isn't little Faabl talking?

"Sōmdin' ahs hopponed froam di impahct wit di owl. Yoa'ahr cōmmunicaytin' wit me, yehs?"

Standing on Koodjuman's knee as she sits cross-legged in the meadow, Faabl nods and the two begin a silent conversation that Koodjuman relays to me.

...

Koodjuman? Yes, I hear you, go on.

...

No, nothing from PeeWee.

...

None of us, no nothing.

"Speak it," Seesterfekt says.

"I didn't sense anything," I say, repeating little Faabl's words through Koodjuman's sensory efforts. "Then, there was intent to harm Tsitsyoos coming from the forest. I was flying toward it. I vanished as we collided and fell to the ground. The owl looked around for me but I was invisible and didn't move. The owl felt fear and confusion and flew away. When I tried to come back, nothing happened. When I tried to call out, nothing happened. Then I realized I couldn't hear anything either. I tried communicating with all of you, but no one heard me, no one but Koodjuman."

Delighted by abundant bird song and the absence of mosquitos and black flies on this dry first morning of summer in the forests of Winhall, the world seems in balance once again. Well, at least my world—the new one I've come to terms with since meeting Seesterfekt Purbits. But their world, the world of the Peepl, seems very much out of sorts.

Chapter 22

A Long Time Coming

June 21, 2018
Summer Solstice
Waxing Gibbous Moon

Third Position of the Solar Year (High Sun Day)
One Day past Seventh Trailing Half Moon

Hmm, 6:07, it's official... But what is it that hinders Old Purbits' thoughts and actions at solstice and equinox?

"It's magnetic," Seesterfekt says, recovering from suspension.

"Magnetic?"

"Yes, it's the Sun's gravity crossing the equatorial plane in spring and fall during your equinoxes, or, as in the moment that just passed, when that gravitational pull stops moving longitudinally on your summer and winter solstices."

"You can feel that?"

"Of course. So can you. It's just that your present-day cultural norms don't allow room for these kinds of forces to be acknowledged for what they are. Instead, you simply reach for a beer, a cigarette, an NSAID or some other more potent diversion to confuse what you're feeling. If you would recognize what's really going on, you'd experience something wonderful every change of season."

I reach for my thermos, remove the cup, and pour. "It's a little early for a beer, but I wouldn't mind a coffee."

Seest gives a headshake. "Exactly."

Mmm, that's good coffee... "You miss them?"

"Yes, but young Faabl PeeWee needs Tsitsyoos and Koodjuman right now. And Saint Lucia is much safer since Trinidad became the focus of search efforts in the summer of 2010."

"Search efforts?"

"Yes, ever since the bird-strike incident, world powers interested in what the Peepl are able to do have finally left Saint Lucia alone. It was a long time coming."

"I understood there was interest in Khetchishsht because of the bird strike on Trinidad, but I didn't know humans were searching for Peepl in Saint Lucia."

Seesterfekt takes a long and thoughtful pause. It's a good moment to top off my cup, and position myself comfortably against a tree.

"Black Caribs were known as violent and cannibalistic," Seest says. "That was their label once certain European powers realized Black Caribs stood in the way of yet another thing they coveted as much as land and gold—the power to vanish and reappear. Maybe even fly. Yes, my friend, prejudice dies hard, and ancient sentiments that

Africans were not of original blood on this continent, smoldering for thousands of years, quickly reignited in the fury for dominance brought across the Atlantic: Colonial expansionism built on countless lives trafficked from Africa."

"I've done a little reading about the island's history, but so little is recorded before 1500."

"Yes," Seest says, nodding, eyes gazing into the past. "That's when the colonial-era battle for Saint Lucia really began—in 1499, when a well-known navigator and cartographer from Spain by the name of Juan de la Cosa etched an island on his chart of the Caribbean. He named it El Falcón. It was the bird you call the broad-winged hawk that inspired him. Circling overhead as they passed near the island, it was the first animal he and his crew saw that day."

Not a seabird?

"No my friend. The wind was from the east in the morning. Most seabirds were gathered on the lee side of the island in calm-water coves. The broad-winged, floating on thermals generated by the interior mountains, simply tipped its wings this way or that to glide out along the shoreline and back."

How does Seesterfekt know all this?

"Stop thinking so loudly and let me continue," Seest says, smiling.

"Sorry."

"A few years after Juan de la Cosa returned to Europe with his new chart, El Falcón was renamed by the religious hierarchy in the Vatican. Only after being renamed was it allowed to appear on the official Vatican globe of the known world."

"Saint Lucia?"

"Yes. Everything named in those days had something to do with either the religious or the royal: Synonyms for the same power-hungry mindset." Seesterfekt laughs.

"So what battle took place in 1499?"

"You don't listen well sometimes," Seest says, deadpan. "Have I ever told you that?"

"Huh?"

"What battle? Who ever said there was a battle?"

"But you said the battle for Saint Lucia began—"

"In 1499, when a well-known navigator and cartographer from Spain by the name of Juan de la Cosa etched an island on his chart of the Caribbean?"

"Yes, exac—"

"So what battle are you referring to?"

I wonder if this is what it feels like to be tasered. "Ok, ok, my mistake. Can you just continue?"

"I was continuing, until you interrupted me with your silly question."

Now who's being silly?

"What's silly," Seest says, with a broad toothy grin and a wink, "is that for fifty years, Spain was unchallenged by other colonial powers in the waters around Saint Lucia."

"Jambe de Bois," I say, remembering the name from some of the history I read.

"Yes! A sturdy fellow of Rus blood. He and his men attacked passing Spanish ships from the north end of the island."

"Pirates?"

"They were called privateers back then. As with mercenaries now, shameful deals were made with those who got things done, when politics rendered kings and potentates unable to."

"The Caribs didn't consider Jambe a threat, did they?"

"No, they didn't. History notes that. The Caribs only knew that Jambe and friends were keeping others away from the island. What history doesn't note is that the privateers had a temporary agreement with other colonial powers, hoping to thwart Spain's ambitions in Saint Lucia."

"Pigeon Island, in the north. They staged their raids from Pigeon Island."

"Yes, Jambe had little interest in anything Lucian beyond little Pigeon Island. Except for a few young Lucian women, who, as the stories go, were quite enamored by his wooden leg."

"I don't remember that." I laugh. "But I do recall reading something about Dutch settlers arriving in the south... Some decades after Jambe's mercenaries left Pigeon Island?"

"Yes, Black Caribs quickly eradicated them, and a few years later, English settlers tried the same thing. They too were killed or driven off. Tales were told by survivors reaching Venezuela, of Christian men, women, and children being massacred for the sake of little beings with miraculous powers living on the island. For a time, few righteous, 'god-fearing' European settlers from other islands ventured to Saint Lucia."

"I remember something about survivors and Venezuela, but I certainly don't remember reading anything about little beings with miraculous powers."

"No. That's not part of recorded history. But after thirty years of this story circulating in the Caribbean, the English sent the largest group to date with three hundred settlers, hungry for a new life in paradise, unafraid of tall tales of little beings."

"Why does this sound like a recipe for disaster?"

"Because it was. Though the Black Caribs had been less aggressive with the trifle numbers of settlers arriving in the previous few decades, most of these new settlers arriving on the island were imbued with the Imperial hubris Caribs loathed. The settlers were—as the English used to say often about their dealings with natives—quickly dispatched."

“It must have been after that, but wasn’t the French West India Company involved in Saint Lucia on some level?”

“Yes, around fifty years later, the French West India Company was trickling settlers onto Saint Lucia with little resistance from the Black Caribs.”

“Really?”

“Yes. It seems as though French arrogance was more agreeable to the Caribs than English hubris, so there was no large-scale slaughtering. Though the Caribs did, on occasion, raid certain settler’s homesteads who either knowingly or unknowingly insulted them in some way. Entire family’s lives depended on what they had to give as gifts of reparation. And of course the mood of those leading the raids.”

“Sounds like a tenuous peace.”

“At best. Until a military officer, representing the Company in negotiations with the Caribs, took one of their women as a wife.”

“Uh oh!”

“No, no,” Seesterfekt says, with a headshake and a finger wag. “It’s not what you think. She was offered to him as a gift—an offering he thought might guarantee the peace he believed they had agreed on.”

“Mistakenly believed?”

“Yes, it was the only reason he accepted. The woman had been passed over numerous times by suitable Carib men because of a certain rumored propensity she had for not bathing. If he wanted to secure the peace, he had to take her. Refusing would have been an insult." Seesterfekt laughs. "He was outmaneuvered by the Caribs on this one. The offer of a wife was not only sure to make the peace agreement binding..." Seest laughs harder. "It was the only way the father of this bride would ever get her out of his home!"

"Not bathing?"

"Very disagreeable to the Caribs," Seest says, smiling. "But bearable to the French officer, with perfumes and scented oils at his disposal, which, rumor had it, she dowsed herself with several times a day."

"Still," I insist, scrunching my nose as I imagine the malodorous layers of body secretions and perfume. "Surrounded by ocean yet never bathing? Maybe she wasn't right in the head?"

"Exactly! You hit the nail *on* the head. She was rumored to be of fine body, but of ill mind with an ill temper."

"Poor guy," I say, cringing. "High price to pay for peace."

"That's not the end of the story," Seest says, with another headshake. "Having exacerbated the situation by taking a wife he didn't want while still not having the peace he did want, the officer finally offered to purchase the island."

"He did? Or the French West India Company?"

"The Company, of course."

“And?”

“The Caribs, dwindling in number, accepted the offer, this time *they* mistakenly believed the purchase price was assurance that the French would help guard the Peepl against the English.”

“Oh no.”

“Oh yes.”

“I remember reading that something big happened in 1659 involving the English.”

“Yes, you’re right,” Seest says.

“Had the French left by then?”

“No, they hadn’t. You’re a few years ahead of where I am in the history.”

“Sorry. Please, continue.”

“When the officer died several years after purchasing Saint Lucia, the Black Caribs discovered that a number of the French settlers *had been* and *still were* actively searching for the Peepl. Caribs began attacking the settlements again. At first, they went after those directly involved. But distrust grew and they began attacking anyone who either wasn’t Carib, or Caribs who had been welcoming to the French. The island spiraled into chaos and news of it spread throughout the Caribbean.”

“So…” I say. “In 1659 the English invaded hoping to capitalize on the chaos.”

"Yes! Exactly. But the Black Caribs and French somehow refocused their hatred for each other on the English, and repelled them."

"So there really wasn't something significant about 1659."

"Yes, there was. The humiliating defeat set the stage for a bigger invasion in '63, when, with over seventeen hundred men, including many Red Caribs, the English invaded again, this time overwhelming the Black Caribs and the French, restoring honor to the Crown."

"So that was the beginning of the back and forth possession of the island between the English and the French that had, what was it, a dozen exchanges?"

"It was more than that over the next century and a half. The ferocity between the English and French to claim Saint Lucia was obviously unusual at the time, and to this day, it stands out as such for all to see. History recorded that lucrative trade was the reason for exchange of control, but I tell you my friend, what I say is the truth."

"All of this was over the Peepl?"

"Yes, all because of Tsitsyoos and Khetchishsht. They were the only Peepl left in the Great Circle."

"But they were still Koodj—the legend, the vanishing, the flying. It didn't apply to either of them at the time."

"No, it didn't," Seesterfekt says. "But the once-upon-a-time legend is now a vector for scientific study and catalyst for military technological advancement. Your country has been after this knowledge since its inception. Did you think I was kidding about the phrase, We the Peepl?"

"I knew it, god damnit!" I say, hot coffee gurgling from my mouth. "That warm day in February. The day you asked me to go to Saint Lucia. I knew you were serious."

"Of course I was serious. But you were so focused on the answer to why we the Peepl leave conversations the way we do that you didn't have brain space enough to hold that thought and discuss something more important."

I hang my head, embarrassed by the truth.

"We the Peepl," Seest says, sighing, then pausing. "It's a very long story about a very short phrase that fell on deaf ears, but it's a story for another day."

Ugh!

"The old colonial powers fought over this coveted knowledge," Seest says. "Your new Republic sought after it. Even what you called the Third Reich was trying to acquire it."

"What?!"

"Their efforts intensified in May of 1939, when German officer cadets arrived in Saint Lucia to vacation. While enjoying the scenery and gracious hospitality of the island's inhabitants, they were also gathering intelligence: photographing Castries harbor and the small naval and air stations on the island at that time, and mingling with the locals, buying rounds of drinks in exchange for the telling of legends of small beings that could disappear and reappear. It was obvious what the focus of their clandestine mission was. But if there's one thing Lucians don't do, it's betray the trust of the Peepl." Seesterfekt laughs. "Those cadets left the island hungover and unclear about the dozens of misleading stories they were told, none of which corroborated another. At the same time, your Allied intelligence services were trying to find and acquire this legendary vanishing ability that completely eluded the Third Reich."

Seems odd... so much advancing so quickly... pre-World War Two... humans believed in something like vanishing? Huh? What the— "Hey, where are you? Come on, you're not really leaving now, are you?"

"Odd? Really?" Seest says, reappearing.

"Shit! Don't do that just to prove a point. I thought you were gone."

"Gone? You don't believe in something like vanishing, do you?"

"Yes, I do. Now that I know it's not magic."

"Your scientists don't believe in magic either, but they do have interesting theories on the subject of things vanishing. Anyway, humans are willing to believe anything that might secure an advantage when it comes to war."

I take a deep breath, exhale, sip coffee, and nod.

"By August of 1940," Seest says, "seven British possessions had military leases of various-sized parcels issued to your government for ninety-nine years."

"Ninety-nine years?"

"Yes, well, the war to end all wars was only twenty-two years in the past, so looking ahead, ninety-nine years made sense."

"So it's still in force? The US still has leases on seven British possessions till 2039?"

"I believe it's contingent on actual need under the conditions of war only. Now, may I continue?"

"Yes, I'm sorry. These are new things, things I've never heard about."

"The lease on Saint Lucia was the last stipulation of an agreement the US proposed in exchange for an offer of fifty old destroyers instead of twenty-five the British had asked for. The British knew what was at stake on the island, but were allies with your country against a common foe, and Saint Lucia was still the Crown's. Twice the number of destroyers was worth gambling the Americans wouldn't find the 'interest' before the British. After all, hundreds of years had passed and no one ever found so much as a feather."

"So it was a deal?"

"Oh yes. In less than a year, progress was well underway on three thousand acres for an airbase near Vieux Fort in the south, which is now part of Hewanorra International Airport. One hundred twenty acres in Gros Islet for access to the harbor in Castries was also being improved, and a smaller airfield, just south of the harbor, was undergoing improvements as well. Within that same year, a substantial number of off-duty American military personnel wandering the area of the Soufriere Volcanic Complex with packs full of gear—that no one ever saw them take out or use, but which they claimed was of a seismic research nature—sparked local fears that they might be planting mines in the area to thwart an invasion. The British objected to the excursions, sighting that the Soufriere Volcanic Complex was not included in the lease agreement with the US, forcefully requesting all US personnel, off duty or otherwise, stay out of the area."

"That's Tsitsyoos' home—Soufriere—right?

"Yes."

"Was that request honored?"

"No," Seest says. "With such a forceful request, the British might as well have said, 'you're getting warmer.' The exploration of the area continued daily, only now, the mission was carried out at night with increased fervor."

"I've never heard this history before."

"It's not available my friend. And there's more." Seesterfekt stands up, gazing through the leafy green forest. With a sniff of the air, that single nostril opens wide. Finally shrugging, Seest stops sniffing and sits down. "After France fell to the Nazis in June of 1940, formerly French-controlled Martinique, less than fifty kilometers away from Saint Lucia, became a haven for their submarines. One of them, *U-161*, slipped into Castries harbor in the early morning darkness of March tenth, 1942, and torpedoed the ocean liner *RMS Lady Nelson*, and a merchant ship, the *Umtata*. Both were sunk. What history doesn't record is that a fake communiqué was sent as bait saying that the 'interest' had been found and was aboard ship, waiting to leave at dawn that morning. The ploy worked, but the fear of things being worse than expected drove your leaders' decision making after that."

"Worse than expected?"

"Yes. If the Nazis were willing to risk squeezing a seventy-meter-long submarine into an impossibly tight harbor to keep the Allies from acquiring knowledge contained within the 'interest,' it likely meant they were working on theories concerning verschwindende tarnung."

"Wait, what? Gershwin had a turn on?"

Seesterfekt stares at me with a headshake. "Disappearing camouflage. Invisiflage was the American term. The British called it camovanishing. The French, on the other hand, proudly kept the simple name of camouflage, working on the assumption that invisible camouflage was the future, and all other types would be called camouflage with a prefix, describing the material used in the camouflaging such as tree camouflage, net camouflage, mound camouflage and so on."

I shake my head, smiling. "Fascinating."

"Yes, well, the idea was far more successful than the development of it. But fear the Nazis would create an invisible super weapon with this technology—using uranium acquired by seizing Czechoslovakia through appeasement three and a half years prior—prompted the creation of the Manhattan Project on May twelfth, 1942."

"Are you telling me that the Manhattan Project was somehow linked to the Peepl?"

"I'm not telling you that. I don't have to. You just learned it," Seesterfekt says.

"It's a lot of very interesting information, Old Purbits, but how did we end up here?"

"You said you didn't know that humans were searching for the Peepl in Saint Lucia after I mentioned that PeeWee will be better off there with Koodjuman and Tsitsyoos now that the focus is on Trinidad."

"Right, yes."

"But much more importantly, it's another account that illustrates how the Peepl have been woven within the fabric of human history."

A thrush's morning herald weaves through the forest. Seesterfekt stands up, watching leaves wiggle in the breeze. "I'm leaving for Italy."

"What?! Italy? Wait! We barely closed the book on Saint Lucia. What's in Italy?"

"Satcher Ibuton," Seest says, vanishing. "I'll see you there the evening of the eighth whole moon of the year —"

"Wait. What, me?"

"At Vittorio's, west of Valnontey, south of Aosta. Don't be late for dinner." Seest's voice fades amid the rustling leaves. "Alps" is the last word I hear, the rest erased by the winds.

Part Four

No Turning Back

An Airbus 380-800 isn't just the largest commercial airliner in the world, it's a behemoth of engineering miraculousness. The miracle is that it flies at 1.2 million pounds fully laden at takeoff.

As a passenger on the lower level staring at the wing, bent like an osprey's—it took up the entire view outside my window during taxi—I had my doubts. But after rolling down the runway and lifting into the air as though sliding on a silk ribbon—the entire seven-and-a-half-hour flight, portal to portal from New York to Turin being equally smooth—I'm a believer.

But there should be some aviation law exacting penalties against the parents of misbehaving child perpetrators of sleep deprivation during overnight flights. Fortunately, I slept on the one-hour ride from Turin to Aosta.

Chapter 23

Aosta

July 23, 2018
Waxing Gibbous Moon

Four Days past Eighth Trailing Half Moon

The alignment of Arco di Augusto and the ancient walled city of Aosta approached from the east—as one would have if traveling from Rome in AD 25—is at once audacious and arrogant in its attempt to mimic the majesty of the surrounding mountains.

I feel the anxiety of a non-Roman and the relief of one of her own as I pass through the arch, leaving the roar of the glacier-fed Buthier de Valpelline behind. Approaching the Porta Pretoria along Via Sant' Anselmo, memories of a time when this area was free of present-day din and clutter—the sounds of horse hooves, wheeled carts, and sandaled feet—echo between the wall ahead and the arch behind.

Inside the ancient city walls, a short walk reveals the Teatro Romano with four of the nine imposing twenty-two-meter-high sections of its southern façade still standing. Visible through the entryways to the theater, Mont Vélan and Grand Combin in Switzerland lie to the north above cloud-veiled valleys.

Past and present clamor for my allegiance. The enduring mountains, the crumbling structures of man, the vibrant, ever-evolving town alive with residents and tourists alike. It's an irresolvable equation scribbled onto the landscape.

Perhaps the solution lies in the view south from the northwest corner of the theater ruins. Towering 2,542 and 2,959 meters above the ancient city, Becca di Nona and Monte Emilius speak the wisdom of stone in silence. The world is made of rock and only rock endures, despite the toil of those who work it. No wonder the Peepl first form a relationship with rock, water, and wind.

And behind those peaks, in a high valley south of here, lies Vittorio's, and my next meeting with Old Purbits.

At 2,588 meters of elevation, Rifugio Sella, a.k.a Rifugio Vittorio Sella, was a welcome sight approaching from the south after thirteen and a half kilometers and numerous gains and losses in elevation from my starting point earlier today at 1,600 meters in Valnontey. Though the route is a bit circuitous compared to the oft-traveled trail directly west out of town, it's worth every meter in both length and height for the scenery of Parco Nazionale Gran Paradiso. Of course that's easier said after a hot shower, two pints of beer, and three generously sized bowls of minestrone.

Chapter 24

Vittorio's

July 27, 2018—17:00
Full Moon

Eighth Whole Moon

Where's Old Purbits? ... said not to be late for dinner.

And I was right, yes? I hear Seesterfekt's voice in my head, clear as though Seest was standing beside me.

Ok, obviously you're invisible because there are peop... sorry, other humans around. But where are you?

I'm not where you are. But you need to be where I am.

"What?" I blurt, attracting unwanted attention from a couple sitting nearby at streams edge, just below the Rifugio.

Yes, that's why I wanted you to have dinner. Now gather your things and start walking west. Stay on the Alta Via 2. When you reach the junction where the trail for Colle delia Rossa heads north, there's a kink in the trail that takes you south. As the trail turns west again after the kink, leave it, and walk upstream. We'll be there, less than two hundred meters away.

We?

Yes, we. Now hurry, the eclipse will begin soon.

Great... just forget about the bunk I rented... and a little thing called sleep.

Despite the lack of rest, I'm infused with a second wind by the cool evening air, as the comfort of Rifugio Vittorio Sella fades with the view of it in the distance. It's quiet out here. The network of streams this high in the valley flow rather than run.

Silhouettes of Ibex on a nearby hill watch me. They remind me of the shadow creatures of the forests at home.

A nearly full moon hangs low in the east. In the northwest, chalk and blue-gray, beige and brick paint the lower ridges of the Grivola, its shadowed summit tearing jagged lines in a zaffre sky.

Chapter 25

The Geostones

July 27, 2018—21:00
Full Moon

Eighth Whole Moon
continued...

Passing the junction where the Colle delia Rossa trail turns north, I arrive at the kink in the Alta Via 2 that Seesterfekt mentioned. I stop and ponder the meaning of Satcher.

Satcher... the seventh age... the last age... past material existence... revered age... no longer seen or heard from... Embracer of the Unknown... How can I meet who is never seen or heard from?

Leaving the trail where it turns west, I walk toward the stream. It's gurgling water glistens in the moon's fading light as Earth's shadow bounces back, darkening the landscape. My eyes adjust to the slow procession of darkness as I walk along the stream.

"Hello, my friend," Seesterfekt says.

I stop to locate Seest's voice in the fading moonlight.

"Here." Seesterfekt stands motionless on a large stone, curiously positioned in the middle of a triangle of three larger stones. "Few humans ever notice these stones and their arrangement. And very few ever venture in for a closer look. What do *you* see?"

"What I don't see is Satcher Ibuton. I thought you said you were both here."

"Technically, I didn't *say* anything," Seest says, shrugging. "Satcher is here. But I didn't ask you what you don't see, I asked you what you do see."

"Well, they're all terribly worn." I give Seest a sideways glance. "But you're standing on an ovate stone, surrounded by what looks like a geodesic dome directly north of a pyramid, with a rectangular block due east. They're equidistant, seem deliberately the same height, and proportionately sized... There's a good view of the huge glacial shelf below—"

"Yes! That's the key. This is where Koodj Ibuton came to continue forming a relationship with rock, water, and wind. Ibuton formed these stones into beautiful precise shapes with exact measurements and proportions. The shapes you see now are only remnants of what they were."

"Koodj Ibuton? I understood the lack of *s* or *t* suffix when you referred to Ibuton as Satcher, but what was Ibuton's gender before that and why didn't the young Koodj begin a formative relationship with everything that grows and multiplies?"

Seesterfekt looks at the ground. "Well, Ibuton never developed gender," Seest says, then looks out into the darkness. "That Koodj was an anomaly that was never known to have happened before and never repeated since. Without gender, Ibuton had little interest in things that procreated or otherwise multiplied."

The darkness of totality envelopes the landscape.

The stones glow, their shapes defined.

Seesterfekt hops off the ovate stone, which is now growing brighter than the rest.

"Ibuton," Seest says, nodding and blinking slowly. "Tonight, you'll witness the moment in the age of Satcher when past material existence moves to Embracer of the Unknown, also known as the disappearance."

"I didn't realize there were stages as Satcher. I thought it all happened at once."

"It depends on the individual. Satcher Ibuton picked this moment four thousand years ago, when I moved on from the age of adulthood as Seestergohd. Old Satcher wanted to leave during the last of the longest lunar eclipses for me as Seesterfekt, passing on to the next Manthasif, the light of the geostones, preserved in shadow, revealing the precursor to dark energy in the life span of a lunar eclipse."

"Wait-wait-wait." My head quivers. "That was a lot of words I'm not used to hearing, all in the same sentence. Could you translate what you just said into something I can grasp?"

"It's difficult." Seesterfekt scratches that hair-feathered head with all six fingers of the right hand. "You can't grasp the precursor to dark energy before understanding dark energy itself, let alone fathom how light is preserved in shadow."

"You're right, I have no idea what you're talk—"

Seest raises a hand, and nods. The ovate stone's light spreads out within the geostones, revealing the precision of their shapes; each one appears as though it's just been cut and polished to perfection.

It's alive... the ovate stone... I feel it.

Yes. This is dark energy illuminating the stones, channeling through Satcher Ibuton.

But I thought you said the Peepl refer to dark energy as such because you can't see it, only feel it.

Do you feel something now?

Yes, but I see it also, in the stones.

What you feel is the precursor to dark energy. What you see is light. The precursor to dark energy hidden in shadow, creates light. Light, like all energy is waves. Life energy is no different. Light waves precede life energy and the end result of life energy is the return to light, though in the vastness of the Universe, that light is hidden by the shadow of gravity; endlessly compressing it. But dark energy repels gravity and keeps the Universe from collapsing. Every life form, from single-celled organisms to the unfathomable giants of the early galaxies, all create dark energy. Matter, ***as***

***you know it**, is changed and transferred. But dark energy increases dark matter, increasing gravity, pushing back at the precursor. It is, my friend, the Simmering Sphere of Everything, the eternal flux, always seeking balance by sustaining imbalance. Balance would dissolve the Universe and erase time, making everything nothing. These truths escape your science. For now.*

"This is too much Purbits, I'm—" Darkness and silence surround me.

My eyelids fling open. The bright light of the full moon steals my night vision.

"Rest, my friend," Seesterfekt says.

Chapter 26

An Introduction

July 27, 2018—23:00
Full Moon

Eighth Whole Moon
continued...

"What happened, where are we?" I ask, sitting up in the chill night air.

"You passed out," Seest says, looking behind me. "We carried you here."

"We?"

"Yes, we," a feminine voice says behind me.

"Tsitsyoos?" As I turn to greet my dear sister in the bright light of the full moon, I realize there's no mistaking this *isn't* Tsits, unless young Seestergohd Tsitsyoos no longer has wings.

We stare at each other as the silence grows awkward.

"Koodj ZzZzrrrlll-PeePeet," Seesterfekt says. "Meet DedjoTah."

First part of that sounds indigo bunting-ish... "DedjoTah Purbits? Really?"

Seesterfekt laughs.

"You call him that?" Koodj ZzZzrrrlll-PeePeet says. "It's mother needs to clean it after birth?'"

"They don't call me that. No one calls me that. Right?" I glare at Seesterfekt. "It was a joke our friend Koodjuman made back in June."

"Just before Faabl Peewee's emergence," PeePeet says. "Yes, Koodjuman showed me the whole thing. But I didn't realize Teacher actually calls you DedjoTah."

"Teacher doesn't." I glare at Seesterfekt again. "But how did Koodjuman show—"

"Revealing events to one another," Seest says. "As Tsits did with you before Faabl PeeWee's emergence. Think of it as 'live streaming.' Koodjuman showed ZzZzrrrlll the entire event."

"It's as clear to me as if I had been there," Koodj says.

I turn back to the young Koodj. "Do you mind if I call you PeePeet?" I'm unable to make the high-pitched trilling sound of ZzZzrrrlll the way they do. "And this way I'll remember you're male, even with that feminine-sounding voice."

"EXCUSE ME?"

What did I—

"You should be aware that I have no gender distinctive suffix added to my name."

"But 'PeePeet'—that ends in a *t* sound, denoting you're a male Koodj."

"ZzZzrrrlll-PeePeet is my chosen name from the calls of snow finches I heard as bulb, before I emerged—as *female.*"

I give Seesterfekt a sideways glance while scratching my chin.

"About three hundred five kilometers east northeast of here," Seest says, shifting eyes in that direction.

I feel my brow raise and my eyes widen. I stare squarely at Purbits while still scratching my chin.

"Ibuton and I didn't know what to do with her when she emerged as female," Seesterfekt says, gazing at the moon. "Should we give her a suffix at emergence or wait till she reached the age of Koodj? The more time passed, the less important a suffix seemed to be. So here she is. Suffix-less."

Nodding, I turn to PeePeet. "Even in the moonlight I can see you have a post-molt texture to your plumage, but you're Koodj, so were you born—sorry. Did you emerge like that?"

"No, I didn't. The last is the first remember? Only Faabl PeeWee emerged with post-molt plumage. I remain Koodj because I still have gender. But I am fifty-five hundred years old. I would be Seestergohd by now, however I'm only past the *age* of gender, not actually *past* gender even though I molted twenty-five hundred years ago."

I glance back and forth at my companions. "Koodj denotes not past the age of gender and Seest denotes past the age of gender. If I've understood right, these designations are about age, not gender, right?"

"Yes," she says. "But we maintain that although my age in years is beyond Koodj, I'm still not past *my* age of gender, so *I* am *not* Seest."

Awful lot of variations on their theme... a lot of rules that aren't followed... a lot of unnatural occurrences that seem to occur naturally... what were we talking about before—

"What happened at the geostones," Seesterfekt says.

"Yes, what *did* happen there, and where are we now?"

"Come," Seest says, standing up and walking to what appears to be a cliff edge. "They're right down there." Seest points directly south. "Only about three hundred meters away. You see, we didn't carry you very far."

"What did I miss? What happened after I fell asleep?"

"Passed out," PeePeet says, approaching us. "You passed out from the gravitational energy. I jumped under you so you wouldn't hit your head."

"Thank you."

"It was my pleasure," she says, leaning against my leg.

"PeePeet!" Seest barks.

"What? He smells good."

"Wait, what did you say?" I snap, quickly stepping away from her.

"It's been like this from the beginning, I'm afraid," Seesterfekt says, with a headshake. "She doesn't mean anything by it. She's just attracted to mammalian male pheromones."

"Huh. What? Are you kid—"

"Don't worry," she says, looking up into my eyes and reaching for my leg. "Seesterfekt is right. It's just a pheromone thing. Besides, you couldn't handle me."

"Handle you? Listen sister—"

"I'm not your sister, Tsitsyoos is, and if Tsits were here, that young Seestergohd would be ashamed of you."

"Huh? Wha—"

"Yes! Trying to take advantage of an older woman."

I sit on the midnight-chilled ground, shaking my head. Seesterfekt and PeePeet writhe in hysterics.

"Funny, both of you, very funny."

"No man has ever witnessed what you witnessed tonight," PeePeet says, far more serious after a period of calm and silence among we three. "But who knows what the future holds?"

"Actually, at the moment I'm more interested in the past, particularly Satcher Ibuton's past."

Chapter 27
Ibuton's Agenda

July 28, 2018—00:00
Full Moon

Eighth Whole Moon
continued...

By the way, what was Satcher Ibuton's name in the Peepl language?"

My two companions look hard at each other.

"He's learning our language?" PeePeet asks.

"I wouldn't call it learning," Seesterfekt says. "He *is* curious though."

"I am. I'd like to learn, really."

"Waxūgelov Ifexor," PeePeet says, avoiding eye contact with Seesterfekt.

"ZzZzrrrlll," Seesterfekt says.

"Is that the female gender form?" I ask, noting the long *U*.

"I'm impressed," PeePeet says, glancing at Seesterfekt, then back at me. "No, I gave you the pre-gender Earth form since Ibuton's gender was r—"

"ZzZzrrrlll!" Seesterfekt barks.

Closing her eyes, PeePeet nods. "I was teasing. But you're right," she says, looking at me. "Both the female and pre-Earth gender forms have long *U*'s. But the correct form for Ibuton *would* be neutral. What about bird form? Do you understand that?"

"Bird form? You're kidding right?"

Seesterfekt wags a finger. "It's pointless to try to explain to humans who don't have the ability to fully understand birds or conduct meaningful dialog with them."

"But I've made lots of bird sounds in my life. And lots of birds have responded."

"Mimicking is not meaningful dialog," Seest says. "And the birds pity you *sapiens* for doing it. You have no concept of noun forms that express past, present, or future action or state of being, and your vocaliza—"

"But tense is expressed with verbs, not noun—"

"Exactly!" Seest says, with a headshake.

"Just try it. I'll get it." I say, with my best 'gimmie' face.

"Izōrekuha Ahezōt, Yizōjenux Ahezōt," Purbits says.

"The bird form?"

"'It would be Ibuton," Seest says. "Satcher Ibuton. In the *neutral* form."

"Right, well, so..." I swirl my hand horizontally. "About Satcher Ibuton's past..."

"Ibuton emerged in what's known as the Val Camonica," Seesterfekt says, nodding. "In the shadow of the mountain now called Concarena, whose high point is the eastern wall of a glacial cirque. The west wall of that cirque ends at Cimone della Bagozza."

"Exactly how old is Satcher Ibuton?" I ask.

"Once the Peepl reach past material existence, their age is never spoken out of respect," PeePeet says.

"My apologies."

"By that time," Seest says, "the large valley glacier below Concarena had retreated. But alpine glaciers, still connected to each other in the saddles between the highest peaks, remained above all the valleys in the Alps. Rapid climate change caused some of the hanging glaciers to break off in enormous chunks, reshaping the glacial till left behind in the valleys. The weather steadily improved in Val Camonica and other valleys over hundreds of years as it had already in the great plain below."

PeePeet looks southeast through the darkness. "Humans began exploring beyond present-day Lake Iseo during your early Mesolithic Period, but hadn't settled in the Val Camonica yet."

"About ten thousand years ago," Seesterfekt says, "after the danger from hanging glaciers had mostly passed, humans quickly capitalized on the unspoiled ecosystem teaming with food and materials along the length of Val Camonica. Settlement began on the southern shores of the shallow lake, which are now under layers of flood sediment and submerged by the dam at Sarnico. It was the starting point for migration up the valley to Capo di Ponte." Seest pauses. "Remember that these names are not the names humans used back then."

"Yes, of course." I nod.

"The hanging glacier that saddled Concarena, draping to the north and south, posed no threat to Capo di Ponte should it break free as other hanging glaciers had over the centuries. But its water, constantly thundering into the valley below, was easily accessible. From a safe distance, humans would pay homage to what they called Vōzbogtheet."

"Voz bog theet?"

"No. It's one word—a name, Vōzbogtheet. The closest translation in present-day English would be something akin to Water Mountain Deity."

"They etched their emotions into rock on the valley floor," PeePeet says. "Where Vōzbogtheet could see them from above where the water poured off the glacier. The humans believed the deity would be pleased by this and keep the sacred water flowing... It's so funny," she says. "It always has to be something 'sacred' or 'lawful' with humans, otherwise none of you pays attention to it. Why can't most of you observe and listen to reason instead of having to be moved by emotion or coercion. Throughout your history, it's always been a few intelligent ones who let the others know simply what works and what doesn't. It was the elders who came up with the scheme of Vōzbogtheet so they could get everyone to drink the fresh, aerated water thundering into the valley, instead of water from the valley floor. The elders knew that other sources would become unreliable as the population grew. Lifetimes of observation are so easily put to use, yet so easily disregarded with you."

"PeePeet?" Seesterfekt says, copying my gesture of swirling a hand horizontally. "The water?"

"The water? The water..." PeePeet smiles. "Humans there considered the water from Vōzbogtheet sacred and used it only for drinking. Using it for any other purpose was punishable by banishment from the valley. It's no coincidence that Ibuton happened to be there at that time and that the area is known as one of the greatest collections of 'prehistoric' stone carvings in the world."

I shake my head. "I'm not sure I follow."

"Ibuton," Seesterfekt says, "encouraged learning how to etch and sculpt stone. Ibu taught humans to express themselves by creating art from rock. This was foremost on Ibuton's agenda."

"But I thought Ibuton had, how did you put it? '...little interest in things that procreated or otherwise multiplied.'"

"Bravissimo!" PeePeet applauds. "I never understood that either."

"Faabl, Koodj, Seest, Manthasif, and in the end, even Satcher Ibuton all had little interest in humans," Seesterfekt says. "But as Ibuton put it, 'You expect the rock to chip away at itself?' Tapping human emotion was Ibuton's way of trying to make *sapiens* understand that rock is alive, alive in the way that you witnessed tonight."

"Now I understand," PeePeet says. "All these thousands of years it was in front of me, but I never got it."

I squint my eyes and glance sideways at Seesterfekt. "So Ibuton *also* defied convention and broke from The Forbidden."

"No. But look at how much art there is made from stone."

"Are you telling me that Ibuton is responsible for all stone art in the world?"

"Oh no," PeePeet says. "There was Boabodja in Africa, Jinwa in Asia, and Kenekeh in the Americas."

"Didn't you leave one out?" Seesterfekt asks.

"No, there were only four."

"Yes, four. But you only mentioned three."

PeePeet smiles. "Yes, and Ibuton makes four."

"Ah, yes, and now they're all gone," Seesterfekt says, with eyes closed and head bowing.

PeePeet digs nearby, unearthing something. Wiping off the dirt while walking over, she hands me what looks like a broken spear point.

"Everything made of stone beyond the crude tools and weapons of early humans," she says, nodding at the artifact in my hand. "It all began with Ibuton, Boabodja, Jinwa, and Kenekeh. They taught and inspired generations of stone masons and sculptors, builders and artists."

“So they all violated The Forbidden,” I say, wondering if there really ever was such a rule.

Chapter 28

From Corsica to Lago di Vernago

July 28, 2018—in the wee hours
Full Moon

Eighth Whole Moon
continued...

"Of course there was!" PeePeet says. "You forget that *sapiens* have been around a long time and that The Forbidden was put in place for Faabl and Koodj because of a certain branch on your family tree. Ibuton, Boabodja, Jinwa, and Kenekeh were all Seests before contact, so you don't know what you're talking about. The Forbidden was a radical measure forced on us to preserve what was left of our numbers after your *Homo hiedel*-BUTCHER-*ensis* arrived nearly a million years ago and started massacring the Peepl. There has always been contact with humans from the time your ancestors were still pooping from trees!" PeePeet is puffed-out and growling, her eyes as red as a loon's.

I didn't know the Peepl got angry like this.

"Yes, well, it's..." Seesterfekt says. "I'm afraid it's a result of being a very long time with gender. PeePeet gets excited now and again. It's unpredictable and rare, but it happens."

"Yes, it happens!" PeePeet says.

"By the way," Seesterfekt says, turning toward PeePeet. "He's heard the pooping from trees line before."

"Oh, I see," she says, calming, her eyes now obsidian. "Well, during the Neolithic period, early modern humans, the ones you used to call Cro-Magnon, migrated east and south into the Alps from the western plains of Europe..."

How did we get here?

"Clashing and mixing with other humans migrating north and west along the coast into the Alps, this mixed group then clashed with others traveling north across the plain you call Po to the glacial lakes tucked into the Alps, along the north edge of the plain. And when ***those*** three groups weren't ***fighting*** among ***each other***, they joined and ***fought together*** against other humans coming from near and farther east. Yes, ***humans fighting*** all the time. Nothing unusual about ***that***."

"But what *was* unusual," Seesterfekt says, watching PeePeet's rising tension, "was the migration of a teenage girl and her younger brother from the island of Corsica."

I suspect this story has far-reaching implication, and know Seest well enough that the topic of Ibuton, Boabodja, Jinwa, and Kenekeh is closed for now, so I prepare myself for another enlightening Seester-lesson.

"In my seventy-seven-hundredth year," Seesterfekt says, "about fifty-two hundred fifty years ago, in a tiny northern settlement in the area known now as Sisco, twelve-year-old Bēka and her ten-year-old brother Nomōnik used to climb the saddle west of their village to stare out over the water at lands in the east. They could see four islands and a long coastline in the distance, stretching across the entire horizon. But to them, it was all as unreachable as the stars.

"Five years later, sneaking onto the only boat crossing back and forth from present-day Bastia and Toscano to what is now Piombino with sheep, wool, and grain, the two stayed hidden, waiting to escape onto the mainland after dark.

"They stayed in the area known as Tuscany, and provided for themselves by helping large families with small children that were too young to help with the chores of growing crops and tending sheep. Being somewhere new was exciting at first. But the drudgery of every day wore on them till they decided to travel north along the coast, seven years later.

"But as happens with *sapiens*, the man whose family they worked for at the time became enamored with Bēka, who was then twenty-four. He insisted they stay and that she become his second wife. When she objected, a fight broke out between Bēka and the man, who then tried to kill her using an axe with a fine copper head—something of great value he no doubt stole from someone else. Being young and nimble, Bēka evaded him, grabbed the axe, and in a moment of fearful self-preservation, killed the man with one blow to the head. She threw the axe down and ran to get Nomōnik.

It was time to leave. But before setting out, her brother ran back to the barn where the man tried to have his way with Bēka, and took the axe, leaving little evidence as to what had happened.

"Bēka and Nomōnik spent six years traveling along the coast, to what is now Genoa, then across the great plain to the foothills of the Northern Alps at present day Lago di Iseo."

"Lake Iseo—south of Val Camonica, where Ibuton emerged," I say.

"Yes!"

PeePeet nods.

Hmm... what am I sensing...

"By now," Seest says, "many humans had settled along the valley well north of Capo di Ponte, where Ibuton had begun teaching humans to etch their feelings into stone. But that tradition and the one honoring the Water Mountain Deity was forgotten, even though the mountain was still a source of fresh water. Many continued drinking from that source alone, while others drank from any stream or the main river, presently called Oglio, that drains the valley. But the river harbored pathogens from overpopulation further up the valley, and many who drank from it became sick.

"Once again, humans looked to place blame on someone or something, rather than think about the practical consequences of their actions. And unfortunately, the arrival of Bēka and Nomōnik, days before a sweeping wave of sickness, was all the residents there needed to blame these two strangers. They were easy patsies: They looked different, with darker skin, darker hair, slight builds, and they spoke a very different dialect than that of the local tribes."

"Where was Ibuton at this point?" I ask.

"Actually, while all this was happening, Ibuton was very near to here in the valley where Cogne is now, wandering the mountain passes of that era."

"So this is *your* account of Bēka and Nomōnik. You knew them?"

"Yes."

"From Corsica?"

"Yes."

"From childhood?"

"Yes."

"So you were involved in their lives this whole time."

"Yes, yes, yes. Now, may I continue?"

I bow my head and extend my arm.

"Traveling at night over the pass south-southeast of Concarena, Bēka and Nomōnik made their way to the narrow Valle Dorizzio. They settled at the mouth of that valley above present-day Lago d'Idro for another few years, again working for growing families with small children, before wandering north to present-day Tione di Trento."

I smile. “They were telling anyone who would listen, about the Peepl. With you present.”

“It’s as I’ve told you my friend,” Seesterfekt says, wearing a toothy grin. “It began with Ptk, wandering together, explaining that the Peepl were harmless, even benevolent, and there was no reason to fear us.

“Bēka and Nomōnik were well renowned for their support of the Peepl, even though few humans had ever seen one of us.” Seest giggles. “I was present, but kept out of sight.”

What’s going on with PeePeet... so silent...

“From Tione di Trento, Bēka and Nomōnik traveled to the broad valley of the Adige river, past present-day Bolzano and Merano, following the Adige upstream. Exploring a narrow valley north of the river, they came to the area of Lago di Vernago, which of course, was just high pasture back then. This was a slow journey that took five years, but it ended in a place they finally felt comfortable to settle in and live out the rest of their lives. Remember, my friend, at thirty-eight and thirty-six, Bēka and Nomōnik were approaching retirement age back then.” Seest smiles and pauses for a moment.

“But instead of retirement, here is where the real trouble started. A few years after settling in the high valley pasture where they subsisted on sheep, goat, fowl, and whatever they could hunt and gather, news of something unfathomable reached them via a young girl they met and befriended during their stay at the mouth of Valle Dorizzio, eleven years earlier. She was sixteen now, and far from home, having followed rumors and talk of a brother and sister and small 'creature' wandering the mountains and valleys together. Unfortunately, the only people who spoke openly about such things were those who felt suspicion and distrust, never having seen or met the three companions."

"What was her name?" I ask.

"Sivésta." Seesterfekt's eyes close. "She arrived in a deluge during the warmest spring in recent memory, and with barely a moment to greet each other affectionately, she told Bēka and Nomōnik of a bulb that had been discovered and removed soon after being formed."

Shit.

"Yes, I had a similar thought when Sivésta told us."

They killed the Koodjdook! The voice in my head is that of a young girl. "Sivésta?"... *How can I see this unfolding? ... Purbits?... Is this real?*

Yes, it's possible, though I wasn't expecting it. Focus on Sivésta's voice. Let her take you there.

I hear her through the sound of pouring rain. Sivésta's voice is clear... *They killed the Koodjdook! They trapped them moments after molting, wrapping their cold, black-skinned bodies in sheepskins, preventing any light from touching them. They died! They died because of those horrible humans, my kind, my family. I hate them! I hate them!*

"It's too much!" I bark, forcing my way out of whatever place or condition I was in. "It's too much. Whatever that is, I'm not ready for it."

"I was reading Teacher's memory of Sivésta's account, the night she reached the home of Bēka and Nomōnik," PeePeet says, visibly surprised that I read her reading Seesterfekt.

"That explains it," Seest says, turning toward me. "I was certain I was blocking that memory from you."

"But so was I," insists PeePeet.

Both of them now look at me, sensorially conversing in their ancient dialect to keep me from reading either of them.

"Maybe Tsitsyoos' DNA has something to do with it," I say. "Maybe I read PeePeet because she's female and I guess, in a sense, so am I."

"But Teacher is female!" PeePeet says. "So why couldn't you read Seesterfekt's memories directly?"

"Was," Seesterfekt says. "I *was* female. But you're still not past *your* age of gender. He has a point."

"Whatever the reason, can we continue without sensory recollection?"

They nod, accepting my limitation.

"You told him about sensory recollection?" PeePeet says, revealing my choice of words to mean something more than I intended.

"Sensory recollection? NO!" Seesterfekt says, pausing as a cat does when distracted while bathing.

Sensory recollection?... hmm... must be top secret...

Seest's distracted look softens. "Sivésta heard her family members plotting, and followed one of them to the place where they had seen the Koodjdook lying together. But it was a diversion, leading Sivésta away. The Koodjdook were already molting somewhere else under the watchful eye of another."

"Weren't they able to sense that a human was there?"

PeePeet's eyes close. She bows her head. "Yes. But the molt was underway. There was nothing they could do."

"It was that vulnerable moment," Seesterfekt says. "Same as when Wookwahs and I molted, and when Tsitsyoos lay on your lap, helpless."

"Who were the Koodjdook?" I ask. "What were their names?"

"They were Kraqúil-l-lot, a remarkably cryptic calico female, and Ipálinas, a brindle male who looked very much like Tsitsyoos."

"The shed feather-hair, did the humans take that, too?"

"No. Whatever stories they'd heard of the Peepl didn't include the enigma of molt shedding's. Not a strand was taken."

"And fortunately," PeePeet says, her eyes again as red as a loon's, "none was breathed in or absorbed through wounds."

"Would that have been a problem?"

"We don't know," says Seesterfekt, as PeePeet says "Yes!"

"It *didn't* happen and that's all that's *relevant*," Seest says, staring down PeePeet. "But one member of the family returned to the molting place a few hours later, intent on finding the sheddings simply as a souvenir—"

"Yeah," PeePeet sneers, "like a scalp or an ear."

"But the sheddings were gone," Seesterfekt says. "Intrigued by this, the young man—"

"Wait, what young man?" I ask.

"The watchful eye," PeePeet says. "The same one who captured the Koodjdook lying together, wrapping them in sheepskins, killing them. Sivésta's brother, Ūngeshum. He was twenty-one."

"Yes," Seesterfekt says. "Sivésta's brother started digging around the area of the molt to see if he could find some evidence of it in the scree there."

"I'm sorry. Did I miss where this happened while I was caught in that sensory recollection?" I ask, hoping to tease out some detail with my purposeful choice of words.

PeePeet and Seesterfekt shake their heads. They're not taking the bait.

"It happened on the southwest facing scree field of Cornone di Blumone above Valle Dorizzio. About twenty kilometers from where Sivésta lived."

"So the brother dug up the bulb and brought it back to the rest of the family," I say.

"No," PeePeet says. "The brother dug up the bulb and was hit in the side of his head with a rock, thrown from sixty meters away, killing him instantly."

"What? From who?"

PeePeet shrugs. "Sister, of course."

"She hadn't intended on killing him," Seesterfekt says, "but she had no regret either, though the complex emotions reeling within her challenged clear thinking. Theirs was a relationship that for Sivésta, was one of constant vigilance, to keep her brother from taking what he wanted. It happened a few times when they were younger, but from the time Bēka and Nomōnik arrived at the mouth of Valle Dorizzio eleven years earlier, she kept her selfhood secured from Ūngeshum.

"Sivésta wasted no time on indecision. She pushed all emotion aside and took anything of her brother's that might be useful. Frantically pulling handfuls of tall grass to wrap the bulb in, the reality of never being able to return home set deeper than a splintered-bone fish hook as she looked down the narrow valley.

"Getting a head start on family members she knew would follow once her brother's body was discovered, Sivésta traveled over twenty-five kilometers a day for five days through river valleys, mountains and high passes, heading north, finally arriving at the valley where Lago di Vernago is today, where Bēka and Nomōnik had settled.

"Ūngeshum was discovered two days after she left. After matching a smooth rock stained in blood with the cavity in his head, his family realized they knew only one person who could hit almost anything with a good projectile like that: Sivésta. And the fact that they'd both been missing for days was proof enough for them that she was guilty and on the run.

"It took a day to gather their things and decide on a plan. Knowing Sivésta's lasting affection for Bēka, Nomōnik, and those 'creatures,' they decided to follow the path the brother and sister took eight years before, asking anyone they met about the strangers and their mysterious companion. They would find them. And Sivésta as well."

"I'm trying to understand the timeline here, Old Purbits. Didn't we have a conversation last winter solstice, first position of the solar year, and another back in November on that craggy outcrop, when you told me that emergence happens in spring?"

"Yes."

"And wasn't it in autumn that your Koodjdook molted?"

"Yes."

"And didn't Faabl PeeWee emerge in spring?"

"Very late spring, yes."

"So the Peepl molt in autumn and emerge in spring."

"Yes."

"But If I'm hearing right, this bulb's Koodjdook molted in spring, forming a viable bulb in a few hours?"

"Yes."

"And?" *Wait... no... ugh... of course... Everything changes.*

Old Purbits gives me an opposite-eye-bulging wink of approval for arriving at the Peepl's sole assertion.

"It would be a longer, slower trip for Sivésta's family members traveling north along the Chiese river," Seesterfekt says. "But she was still two days journey from Bēka and Nomōnik when her family started out."

Chapter 29

A True Account

July 28, 2018—in the growing wee hours
Full Moon

Eighth Whole Moon
continued...

"When you say family members, who do you mean? How many people went looking for her?"

PeePeet perks up. "Her much older brother, Tōshōl, half-brother Kótki, and twin sister, Olūchka," she says, glaring straight ahead, her eyes reddening again.

"I thought you said it was *rare*?"

"I believe I said *unpredictable* and rare," Seesterfekt says. "It's a sensitive topic. It'll p—"

"You were there, right? With Bēka, Nomōnik, and Sivésta?"

"Yes, of course."

"What did you do? What happened with the bulb?"

"Koodjuman was right about this one," PeePeet says, casting off her darkness and laughing. "Non molto paziente!"

"On the third day after Sivésta arrived, the rains stopped," Seesterfekt says. "We decided to place the bulb high on the ridgeline north of the valley, in a saddle between the two peaks known now as Similaun to the east, and Fineilspitze to the west. The bulb was fully formed soon after molt, but consciousness was delayed. I could sense the bulb was alive, but for the first time in the history of the Peepl, a bulb was not sentient."

"What was that like?"

"You should let Teacher tell the story," PeePeet says.

"What I didn't sense," Seesterfekt says, "was that Tōshōl, Kótki, and Olūchka were camped along the Adige River at the mouth of the valley leading up to the high-pasture home of Bēka and Nomōnik. Because of Sivésta's family's 'notoriety in certain circles,' a man on the periphery of one of those circles, who the siblings sought out on their first day of pursuit, told them where Bēka and Nomōnik lived, how to get there, and exactly how much payment he wanted *before* telling them. It cut their search time to a fraction of what it would have been without this information. Of course, their promise to pay *after* he told them was the death of him."

"Why didn't you sense them?"

"You should let Teacher tell the story," PeePeet says, a little less patient than before.

Seesterfekt's head tilts slightly, lips pursing. "Olūchka. Though she didn't know it, sensory domains were unable to detect her at a distance."

"How far?"

"Ten to fifteen kilometers depending on the lay of the land. In the mountains, on that day, it was ten."

Ten-kilometer lead seems enough—

"Enough for what?!" PeePeet snaps, puffed-out and growling, her eyes as red as a loon's. "Enough to look at the home you finally settled in and know it was about to be burned to the ground?! Enough to reflect on your life and realize it would likely end on that day?! Enough —"

"ENOUGH!" Seesterfekt Purbits thunders.

PeePeet drops to her knees in tears, weeping with emotion so heavy it squeezes sound from the surrounding air, creating the same vacuum silence I felt before meeting Seesterfekt for the first time.

Walking over to PeePeet with outstretched arms, Seesterfekt kneels and embraces her.

They stand together.

Her weeping stops.

The vacuum silence dissipates.

PeePeet nods and Seesterfekt draws a deep breath.

"As the siblings began their ten-kilometer trek up the narrow valley," Seest says, "Sivésta, Bēka, Nomōnik, and I began our fourteen-hundred-meter ascent to the ridgeline, reaching a place in the saddle where snow finches were roosting in nearby cliffs below.

"Sivésta scraped out a hollow in the scree between some larger stones as Bēka, Nomōnik, and I watched a rising smoke plume in the valley burst into flame, engulfing their home in minutes. One by one, the siblings killed every goat, sheep, and captive fowl the brother and sister had. Their world was gone.

"Watching Sivésta gently place the bulb in the hollow she prepared, we had no misgivings about what was to come. After covering the bulb, we all sat nearby talking about humans, Peepl, and what to do next. The bulb was safe—for now. But Sivésta, Bēka, and Nomōnik wanted to face the siblings, who were beginning to climb the unstable cirque face.

"As much as you think I'm often interfering with human interactions, this was one of the countless times I didn't," Seest says, with a headshake.

"Sivésta showed such competence with a bow back at the home of Bēka and Nomōnik that Nomōnik gave her his favorite, taking the latest one he'd been working on for himself, hoping it was adequate. Bēka never shot a bow, but she'd been involved in so many altercations over the years that anything she put her hands on could be a lethal weapon. The three of them agreed to stay with the bulb, not knowing if the siblings were after *it* also, or just Sivésta."

"Wait. You weren't involved at all?"

"When it comes to killing one another, I leave *sapiens* to themselves. You're quite good at it, as you know, and need no help from the Peepl, either directly or indirectly."

Seesterfekt and PeePeet lock eyes. She nods.

"Tōshōl, Kótki, and Olūchka climbed through the darkness," Seesterfekt says, "approaching the saddle directly on that cloudy, fifth day moon night. Olūchka cleared the steep, walking toward Sivésta with her bow on her back, while Nomōnik kept a watchful eye on the ridgeline. Bēka had a flint knife at the ready, but Sivésta lowered her bow as her sister approached.

"Olūchka had no ill feelings toward her sister. As a matter of fact, she was happy Sivésta killed Ūngeshum. Ever since Sivésta resisted their brother after meeting Bēka and Nomōnik, Ūngeshum had turned his focus on Olūchka, almost daily having his way with her. Even the day he was struck down by Sivésta's rock, he had left their encampment only after filling his twisted desire for Olūchka.

"But Olūchka had a twisted psyche of her own, turning anger from her brother's actions into hatred for Bēka, Nomōnik, and the Peepl. And now, she told Sivésta, she was here to kill them. With tears streaming down her face, Sivésta raised her bow once again, steadily aiming at her sister, just a few meters away. Immediately an arrow pierced Sivésta's side, driving through both lungs, dropping her to the ground over where she had placed the bulb just hours before.

"Screaming, Olūchka ran to her sister, holding her up as she sat gasping for air, dying. Another arrow from the same direction struck Olūchka in the chest, ricocheting off a rib, into her heart. Reeling from the shock, she let go of Sivésta, trying to stand, but staggered and spun, falling on top of her.

"Bēka and Nomōnik had dropped to the ground when they heard the first arrow fly. Signing to each other where they believed the arrows were coming from, Nomōnik loosed a shot in the direction they agreed on, but his arrow missed its mark. Hope wasn't enough—the new bow wasn't ready.

"They realized that Sivésta's siblings were unaware of the bulb, and that they were there solely to kill all of them. Bēka and Nomōnik decided to run the ridgeline west, hoping darkness would work in their favor.

"In a one-kilometer sprint they each played back their own memories of their lives together. It was incredible to both of them how fast their lives had passed. Stopping to rest, completely winded, they stayed on their feet close to the cliff edge, breathing quietly, listening for any sound of someone following them.

"Hit in the back with an arrow, Nomōnik gasped for air, falling forward toward the edge. Catching movement out of the corner of his eye, he reached back and grabbed the stone blade of Tōshōl's knife, keeping it from cutting Bēka's neck.

"Bēka rebounded from ducking out of the way, and took advantage of Tōshōl's strength as he stood upright and steady—despite Nomōnik's effort to pull him to the ground—running her knife up the inside of one leg and down the other, along his femoral arteries. Throwing Nomōnik to the ground, and bleeding profusely, Tōshōl lunged at Bēka, who crouched very near the cliff edge. Quickly moving sideways, she watched him disappear into the darkness below. Nomōnik lay on the ground bleeding, but they both knew that Kótki was still somewhere out in the dark.

"After helping Nomōnik to his feet, the two staggered a few hundred more meters along the ridgeline where Nomōnik finally collapsed. Sitting him up, Bēka tried pulling the arrow out carefully, but the stone head worked loose as she slipped the shaft from his body. If the loss of blood from his hand and the arrow wound didn't kill him soon, the infection from the arrowhead was sure to over time.

"Walking to the edge of the ridgeline, waiting for dawn, Bēka heard and saw a shadow racing out of the darkness toward Nomōnik, passing him with speed, and striking his head hard with a stone axe. The shadow approached Bēka, and she could see it was Kótki as he leaped, axe overhead, screaming obscenities. Bēka leaned toward the cliff edge, grabbed Kótki's axe-wielding arm, and using her own weight and his momentum, took them both over the edge."

Seesterfekt and PeePeet are silent, their heads bowed, their eyes closed.

I stare at PeePeet... *Look at me PeePeet... look at me...*

PeePeet raises her head and turns toward me, opening her tear-filled eyes.

"It's you, isn't it? And you carry them both."

"Yes, I was that bulb. And yes, I carry them both. It's the reason I emerged as female. I absorbed Sivésta's and

Olūchka's DNA when their blood washed through the scree during heavy rains, altering my hormonal balance."

"Is that dangerous?"

"Oh, you mean the red eyes, the growling?" Seesterfekt says. "Well, it's, eh, as I said before, PeePeet gets excited now and again. It's unpredictable and rare, but it happens."

"Yes, it happens," PeePeet says, calmly. "May I, Teacher?"

Seesterfekt nods.

"Villagers from the valley below," PeePeet says, "drawn by the fire at Bēka and Nomōnik's settlement the day before, found the broken bodies of Tōshōl, Kótki, and Bēka near the bottom of the cirque that morning.

"Drenching rains, more than anyone had remembered happening before, continued for days. When the skies cleared, a small group returned to where the villagers had found the bodies. Following the washed-out tracks laid down days earlier, they found Sivésta and Olūchka on the ridge where they died, lying face to face over my bulb. These kind villagers piled stones as a monument next to the girl's bodies before carrying them down to burn them, as they had the others. To this day, the location remains marked, though no one who visits or works at Rifugio Similaun or Similaun Hütte has any idea of what happened there.

"Nomōnik's body was only thirteen hundred meters away, but when they found the two girls, the small party of searchers decided that something 'evil' had happened to Nomōnik, something no doubt having to do with the 'creature' rumored to live there, and he was labeled a murderer. No one ever saw him again, and for a human lifetime, no one went up to that ridge. When I emerged through a blanket of snow six lunations later, there was no sense of humans anywhere and Nomōnik's body was already buried by windswept snow."

"Snow that continued throughout the seasons for hundreds of years after," Seesterfekt says. "The body and legend of Nomōnik the murderer disappeared beneath the snowpack."

"Until it was discovered just before fourth position of the solar year, in your year 1991," PeePeet says.

"Wait-wait-wait! What are you talking about?"

"Your Ice Man found near the border of Austria and Italy. Nomōnik is your Ice Man," Seesterfekt says.

My mouth is agape, my breathing paused.

"He has trouble with his jaw sometimes," Seest says.

PeePeet stares at me. "I see... and his breathing."

"Nomōnik was my friend," Seesterfekt says, kick-starting my respiration. "We told you this story in detail for that reason. If you want to tell it, go ahead. But be accurate. Tell only what we've told you—a true account. Don't add or subtract anything. It didn't matter for a very long time because the legend had disappeared with the body. But since the day Nomonik's body was found, I've wanted his story told."

"Yes," PeePeet says, shrugging. "Tell it. No one will believe you anyway."

Hypothermia descends with the cold of early dawn. Without a word, PeePeet walks over and sits in my lap, instantly belaying my shivers. Together, we stare at the potent-white moon, low in the southwest.

Chapter 30
The Wielding

July 28, 2018— 04:30
Full Moon

Eighth Whole Moon
continued…

"By the way, how did you two carry me three hundred meters? And what happened at the geostones after I collapsed? You never told me."

"Well, it really wasn't we who carried you," PeePeet says. "Remember the Ibex you saw on your way here?"

"Yes."

"Seesterfekt suggested they follow you at a distance. When you collapsed, they had just arrived. That large female down there," she says, pointing toward the geostones, "she was the one who carried you."

"They didn't spook from the light of the geostones during the eclipse?"

"Ibex are far less afraid of such things," Seesterfekt says, "than they are of what humans have done to them over the last several centuries. It was more difficult to convince that old nanny to carry you up here than it was for her to stay for one last visit with Satcher Ibuton."

"They knew each other?"

"Yes, cordially. Now, as far as what you missed at the geostones... At the moment you collapsed, Satcher Ibuton's last discernable presence in the realm of the immaterial ended—"

"Wait. Discernable presence in the realm of the immaterial?"

"Not a good time to ask," PeePeet says, shaking her head. "It's... involved."

"Quite," Seesterfekt says. "So the long and short of it is that Old Satcher entered the final phase in the last age of the Peepl: disappearance. So you really didn't miss anything my friend. Ibuton is now an Embracer of the Unknown." Seesterfekt sits down next to PeePeet and me, we three gazing at the geostones in the low light of a new dawn. "Our very existence makes no sense, yet here we are—"

I raise my hands. "Wait. Purbits. What do you mean?"

"With all the knowledge the Peepl have amassed over tens of millions of years, still, why we exist makes no sense."

"What are talking about? What does this have to do with Satcher Ibuton?"

"Ibuton? Nothing. Who said anything about Ibuton?"

I look to PeePeet for help. She shakes her head and laughs. "Keep up," she says. "New topic."

"As I was saying," Seesterfekt says. "Our very existence makes no sense, yet here we are. With all the knowledge the Peepl have amassed over tens of millions of years, still, why we exist makes no sense."

OK, I'm in... "But if I understood you at the geostones, life exists to keep the Universe from collapsing in on itself?"

"And?"

"And the Universe continues."

"And so what if it didn't? Would you know it?"

"Shouldn't I be the one asking such questions and you the one shining the light of reason?" I say, looking to PeePeet for confirmation.

"Reason!" Seest barks. "What is reason but a way of pretending to understand?"

"Are you having some sort of crisis?" I ask, feeling the chill of dawn as PeePeet leaves my lap for a nearby boulder, and leans against it.

"I'm challenging you to open yourself to another gift my friend," Seesterfekt says.

"I don't understand."

"By letting go, by questioning, by accepting that you know nothing."

"Honestly, with what I've heard and seen tonight, I feel like I *don't* really know anything."

Awash in dawn's glow, PeePeet stares at me from her boulder lean-post, arms crossed in a body posture bristling with anticipation.

Our eyes lock.

Peripheral vision fades.

The usual ringing in my aging ears stops.

Pzlamwox...nvhguryt...laksncie...

Did you hear that?" I ask PeePeet.

"Hear what?"

"The voices."

"What voices?"

Mbxa...ljdirhb...wopihsbbyt...qhg...kjaprbidh...

"There they are again. Don't either of you hear that?"

"What are the voices saying?" Seesterfekt asks.

"I have no idea what they're saying. It's sounds, syllables, gibberish."

"Where are they coming from?" PeePeet asks, still propped against the boulder.

"Over there—north. Over there—south. There! There! There!" I say, pointing in all directions. "Everywhere!"

"You think it's possible?" PeePeet asks Seesterfekt.

"It's possible."

"It *was* the whole point of this," she says.

"Yes. But he's got a long way to go."

"Is what possible?" I snap. "The point of what? Where am I going now? What are you two talking about? Did Ibuton do something to me?"

"Ibuton didn't *do* anything," Seesterfekt says. "You were exposed to the precursor to dark energy and have begun assimilating it. It's what we the Peepl carry with us. The domains are made of the precursor. It's what you now carry with you. All life exists as dark energy, but to wield the precursor to dark energy within life is something only the Peepl have done. Until recently."

"What you're hearing," PeePeet says, "are the voices, the thoughts, the minds of everything around you. For now, it's only sounds, syllables. Gibberish as you call it. But in time, you'll begin discerning more clearly. It'll be like the progressive effect Tsitsyoos' DNA has had on you, but this time, everything that's alive will be open to you. Tutto ciò che vive!"

Fear of the unknown grips me. "I'm not sure my mind can handle this amount of input. It's unnatural to the human brain."

PeePeet smiles, shaking her head. "But it's not unnatural for *your* brain. Tsitsyoos gave her love to you with her brindle plumage on Gros Piton. Her love made certain you'd be ready for this day."

I finally understand the bigger plan I've unwittingly been a part of.

"My emotion for you does not have a word in any of your languages." It's what Tsits meant on the fifth day moon... And on the sixth whole moon... "Your fate on this planet is not sealed, yet. But to survive you will need to evolve beyond your human limitation for understanding. And you verify this limitation by calling 'altered' what we call gifted."

"Yes. gifted my friend," Seesterfekt says. "First with the Peepl DNA. And now with The Wielding."

The eastern sky, awash in fuchsia, casts a warm glow on the surrounding open woods, where chlorophyll-starved maple leaves float onto the forest floor. It's sunset on the last day of summer in Winhall, Vermont.

Seesterfekt and I share company with several tree frogs peeping to one another throughout the wood. A few sticks of striped maple burn blue-green as evening's chill pushes against our modest fire.

Chapter 31
Unexpected and Unknown

September 22, 2018—18:49
Waxing Gibbous Moon
Three Hours before Autumnal Equinox

Fourth Position of the Solar Year
Two Days before Tenth Whole Moon

"It's been a year, my friend," Seesterfekt says.

"Yes, I was just thinking that."

"No you weren't. That's my thought."

"Hmm, so it is." I ponder the subtle difference between having my own thoughts and reading someone else's, while eavesdropping *Hyla* dialog.

"Your thought is that it's been almost two months since The Wielding. And you're wondering how PeePeet is and what she's doing."

"Hah, yes, it's true, but I'm also wondering how to manage all this input. Wielding the precursor seems an insurmountable task."

"But you've already filtered gibberish into discernable thoughts. And syllables have become words and sounds that you understand. And most importantly, you've developed the ability to quiet all of it. You're doing well. Only Koodjuman and you have done this."

"So that's what you meant in Italy when you said, 'Wielding the precursor of dark energy within life is something only we the Peepl have done... *until recently*.' PeePeet gave me a clue as well, but I completely missed it. She said, 'No *man* has ever witnessed what you witnessed tonight.'"

"Yes, September twenty-eighth, 2015, on Gros Piton, during a long total lunar eclipse—though not quite as long as the one just passed. It was the night Satcher Shymee Quivistht Pipod Ojeenoaka moved from past material existence to Embracer of the Unknown."

"Shiny quiver pea pod who?"

Seesterfekt laughs. "It's a few phrases from the song of an extinct bird that lived in what you call the Patagonia region of South America, where Faabl Shymee emerged. Back then, it was customary for the Peepl to use longer names than when I emerged. Actually Shymee Quivistht Pipod Ojeenoaka was one of the shorter names of that time. Many had five, six, and even nine names. And there was one Faabl that emerged with thirteen names from four different animals which the poor bulb couldn't discern as being separate." Seest laughs again.

In the absence of bird song and insect-wing din, frog song echoes through the wood. At least that's all I would have thought *before* The Wielding. But they're not singing. They're planning for winter, telling each other where they'll be and discussing which signs to wait for till emerging in spring. Apparently, they have this conversation every year. But every year it's different.

I pull a Chimay Red from my pack. "We've come a long way from our first meeting."

Seesterfekt's eyes shine iridescent green, like a whitetail's at night. "Yes, we have my friend, a very long way indeed. But not quite as far as you and Koodjuman."

"You mean The Wielding?" I shake my head, place a small stick on the fire, then untwist the cork wire from the bottle.

"No, actually I meant you've come a long way to reunite your blood line."

Popping open the bottle, I offer it. "Teacher?"

"No-no, you first," Seest says.

Tang and mellow tickle my mouth as the first swig swirls past my tongue. "What are you talking about?" I extend my arm, offering the bottle again.

"Your ancestors trace back to the same mother living in western Africa, seventy-five thousand years ago," Seest says, reaching for the bottle.

"What?" My arm retracts. "I've read somewhere that *all* living humans come from a limited number of females that long ago."

"Maybe that's true and maybe it's not," Seest says, arms outstretched, waiting for me to extend my arm again.

"But you are the only two humans left of that line. Your DNA is hers, and some from hers mixed with ours during an attempt to save a molting pair attacked by two members of a neighboring human clan, killed in a vicious fight."

I hand the bottle to Seesterfekt. "You're losing me Purbits."

"Then keep up," Seest says, swigging. "Strands of DNA from the molt found their way into that bloodline through wounds received in the fight. And this DNA passed to twin daughters carried at that time, very early in the pregnancy." Seest takes another swig and hands the bottle back.

"What was her name, the woman defending the molting pair?"

"Kirū."

"And her daughters?"

"Tombī and Fūti."

I down a swig, pausing to ponder. "I can't help but notice that human twins—Tombī and Fūti—carried Peepl DNA from a molting pair who were killed, and another set of human twins—Sivésta and Olūchka—passed human DNA to PeePeet in bulb, who's Koodjdook had also been killed."

"Yes." Seest nods. "But now you're getting ahead of me."

I down another swig, then hand the bottle back. "We're all related, aren't we? Kirū, Tombī, Fūti, Sivésta,

Olūchka, PeePeet, Tsitsyoos, Khetchishsht, Koodjuman, me. All related somehow, aren't we?"

"You're not as dumb as you look young fellow, have I ever told you that?" Seesterfekt says, double swigging.

"This is going to take a while, isn't it?" I ask, getting up to relieve myself.

"Yes, go do that." Seest stares at a nearly whole moon gracing the eastern sky an hour after sunset.

The scent of fallen leaves and their crispness underfoot herald the first spate of autumn weather. I add a few sticks to glowing embers after returning. Anxious to hear the story unfold, I give a 'ready' nod to Seesterfekt who hands the bottle back.

"Are you kidding me? It's gone! Really? Next time, you're buying."

"I'm sorry," Seest says, shrugging. "But I'm going to need it."

"Huh?"

"All of what happened was unexpected and unknown, prior to it happening, though I suppose that sounds a bit redundant. Human and Peepl DNA had come in contact before Kirū, Shymee, and Ibuton, but this was the first time involving *Homines sapientes*." As soon as it entered Kirū's blood stream, the Peepl DNA went dormant, yet seemed to be sentient, doing deliberate things."

"That's contradictory. Dormant, yet doing deliberate things?"

"Yes, that's what happened," Seest says, matter-of-factly.

"I don't understand," I say, shaking my head, donning a bulldog-puss. "What did Ibuton have to do with any of this?"

"Shymee Quivistht Pipod Ojeenoaka, or Koodj Shymeet at the time, molted with Koodj Ibuton—"

"STOP!" I'm completely confused. "You just told me that Shiny quiver pea pod —"

"Shymee Quivistht Pipod Ojeenoaka."

"Yes, whatever! ...moved from past material existence to Embracer of the Unknown on September twenty-eighth, 2015. But now you're saying that, he, Koodj Shymeet, was killed seventy-five thousand years ago—"

"Yes."

"I'm not finished!"

"Ok."

"—with Satcher, I mean Koodj Ibuton, who just two months ago moved from past material existence to Embracer of the Unknown right in front of me—"

"Yes."

"Shush! I'm still not finished."

"Ok," Seest says, grinning.

"—and who encouraged humans to etch and sculpt stone ten thousand years ago. *Teaching humans to express themselves by creating art from rock was foremost on Ibuton's agenda.* Those are your words god damnit. Aren't they?"

"Yes." Seest's grin grows.

"But now you're saying that Shymeet and Ibuton were killed seventy-five thousand years ago during molt?! What the hell?"

"Yes," Seest says, with a big toothy smile. "Both Ibuton and Shymee materialized after being killed as though they had just vanished for a while. Only they know how it happened and the secret remains with them somewhere in the Unknown. *Sapiens* might call it a miracle. For us, it's just another example of how change altered everything and now there is anything."

"Wait. What? What did you say?"

"Change altered everything and now there is anything. It's the original version of *everything changes*, proving in fact that it does indeed. And a further example of this is that neither Ibuton nor Shymee could vanish after rematerializing postmortem, which proved to be very disadvantageous at times." Seesterfekt laughs.

What the hell is Old Purbits talking about...

"I'll give you a moment," Seest says.

You know what... sometimes... it's just... I can't... "UGH!"

"Ok, ok," Seest says. "Change was what happened when the Universe began. Now, because of that, anything else *is*. Or to put it succinctly—Everything changes."

"Why do you do that?! Why do you derail conversation that way, with unrelated factoids and useless information."

"Some *sapiens* would call it a miracle. For us, it's just another example of how everything changes," Seest says, deadpan.

"Thank you!" I'm fuming. *Where the hell was I... Right...* "But isn't that well beyond the age of the Peepl: seventy-five thousand years? And I thought you said Ibuton had no gender?"

"Well," Seesterfekt says, "if you go by what happened, no, I guess seventy-five thousand years is not well beyond the age of the Peepl, at least not *those two* Peepl—"

Oy...

"—and Ibuton, like ZzZzrrrlll PeePeet, was somewhat of an anomaly in that even though what had come to be expected as gender norm didn't occur, there was still a molt. Ibuton and Shymeet lay together because their time converged. Not to produce a bulb."

"So how is it we're all related?" I ask, overriding my acute flabbergastitis.

"Shymeet's DNA collected in Tombī, and with it went the Peepl equivalent of human Y chromosome. Ibuton's DNA collected in Fūti, and with *it* went what would be identified as human XX combination, but this was something new for the Peepl. We have only had what you would identify as X and Y chromosomes and combinations. Ibuton's XX combination was neutral. It didn't affect the Y or X in any way."

"My knowledge of this topic is limited. But isn't a pairing of X chromosomes needed to produce a female?"

Seesterfekt smiles. "Yes, your knowledge is limited. With the Peepl, it's simpler. You just need the human equivalent of an X and a Y to create a bulb. The gender of that bulb is determined from environmental factors during the thousand-year length of the age of Faabl. No Peepl emerges with a predetermined gender. Well, until ZzZzrrrlll PeePeet, of course. Other than she, it's always come about quite randomly."

"Go on..."

"Shymeet's DNA continued unchanged, carrying his Y chromosome through forty thousand years. At that point, for a reason we don't know, an XX combination replaced the singular Y for another thirty thousand years. That XX chromosome then passed through Sivésta, dropping one of the pairing which then passed to PeePeet unchanged. During the same timeline, Ibuton's DNA continued unchanged, carrying the anomalous XX combination for forty thousand years. Then that XX suddenly dropped one of the pairing, again, for a reason we don't know, and was carried for another thirty thousand years, passing through Olūchka to PeePeet, again, unchanged."

I raise my arms as if surrendering.

Seesterfekt stops talking and raises an arm, gesturing as though tossing out a handful of seed in slow motion.

"So PeePeet received two separate, single, non-paired X Peepl chromosomes?" I ask.

"Correct," Seest says, with an opposite-eye-bulging Ata Boy! wink and smile. "But by the time PeePeet reached molt, twenty-seven hundred years later, Ibuton's DNA re-altered the X chromosome she'd received from Ibuton through Olūchka, back to the original XX combination."

"And the X from Sivésta?" I ask. "Did Shymeet's DNA re-alter that to a Y chromosome?"

"No," Seest says, shaking that black-plumed head. "But after passing to Khetchishsht from PeePeet, it converted to another XX combination."

"All this converting and dropping of chromosomes—and you don't know why or how?"

"It's as I told you before, as soon as the Peepl DNA entered Kirū's blood stream, it seemed to be sentient, doing deliberate things."

"You also said dormant."

"Yes. Dormant in that nothing was happening directly to the carriers. Only to the DNA itself..." Seesterfekt pauses. "Where was I? Ah, yes. So. When the XX combination passed from PeePeet to Tsitsyoos remained unchanged, it appeared as though the hope of seventy-five thousand years was gone."

"Hope?"

"Of regenerating the DNA before both Manthasifs Shymee and Ibuton became embracers of the unknown. There is a very old saying among the Peepl that translated into English loses some meaning. But I tell you, my friend, it's a serious matter."

"Can I hear it?"

"Probably." Seesterfekt shrugs. "Your hearing's not that bad."

"May I?"

Seest winks.

"Before the Two are Gone Forever,

You together must endeavor,

To bring about a Whole New Age,

The Two must step out from their Cage,

But danger lurks in blending Kind,

So Watch Long first and Know Their Mind."

Staring into Seesterfekt's eyes, "enlighten me," I say, shaking my head.

"The first 'Two' has a double meaning in our language. 'Two' here means two specific individual Peepl, *and* two Kinds, of which Peepl are one.

"'Gone Forever' also has a double meaning; as in individual Embracer of the Unknown, never to be seen again, *and* the loss of a kind, or in this case both kinds.

"'You,' beginning the second line, is a direct reference to the second meaning of the first 'Two.'

"'Whole New Age' is very broad. It could mean length of age of an individual, or a collection of individuals. It could mean age as in another age of the Peepl, other than the ones we already have. Or 'Whole New' as one meaning, paired with 'Age' might mean something altogether different.

"The second 'Two' also refers to the second meaning of the first 'Two,' two kinds.

"'Cage' is the nearest meaning to a word that represents the Ancients' sense of confinements, specifically those of DNA.

"'Kind' is simple; you and I my friend, are different 'Kinds.'

"'Watch Long' goes back to our ancient dialect. It's similar to sit long, but more a variation of the word Peepl, which if you remember means, Watcher Wandering Alone. Watch Long represents tens of millions of years of observation.

"And finally, 'Know Their Mind,' represents something more direct in our language—physically becoming one with the mind of the 'Kind.' This wasn't really understood till Khetchishsht's DNA knit with Koodjuman's corpus callosum, then confirmed when Tsitsyoos' DNA knit with yours."

I raise my arms again.

Seesterfekt is silent.

"But there was one before us," I say. "The young man who was present at your molt: Eyingamyus. Tsits said Koodjuman and I were the first *since* the capture of Wookwahs. And Koodjuman said Eyingamyus told the Olmec leaders he had ability given by the black feathered Gohds to read minds, so he must have breathed in your combined DNA during the molt."

"It's true my friend, that Eyingamyus appeared to read the leaders minds, but all he read was our thoughts, and not always clearly. He'd developed a sense of the Peepl, the strongest in my lifetime. But the Peepl DNA never knit with his corpus callosum. He was perceptive and insightful, and very intelligent, but maniacal and narcissistic, and a zealot as well. He was not the true human being I thought he was. I was mistaken about that one. Tsitsyoos believes Eyingamyus was killed before the full effect of the DNA knitting took hold. Koodjuman was simply recounting what happened. And I believe he was killed just in time to keep yet another human tyrant from sending others to their death in the name of whatever power they themselves wish to hold."

Seesterfekt stares at the ground, lips pursing, then relaxing, then pursing, then relaxing.

I remember the exchange Seest and I had after the story of Ptk... *"Some humans can be trusted," Old Purbits said... And some simply cannot...*

Seest shrugs, looks at me with pursed lips, then relaxes with a deep breath. "I thought Shymeet's and Ibuton's chromosome strands might rejoin, ending the DNA dormancy upon entering PeePeet's bulb in that tragedy on the mountain. When *that* didn't happen, I hoped returning the Peepl DNA to two of the Peepl through PeePeet might be the solution. When it was her time, I sent PeePeet to Saint Lucia to molt. It was a peaceful time there, long before any Europeans crossed the Atlantic. It had become a favorite molting destination because of its isolation and the protections of the Black Caribs and Tsitsyoos' 'kitties,' as young Seestergohd calls them, though they've been protecting the Peepl during molt in the Great Circle for a hundred thousand years.

"Both Tsitsyoos and Khetchishsht were young Faabl's back then, barely half a century old. They stayed with PeePeet atop Gros Piton when she molted, but still, the Old Ones' DNA remained dormant.

"It would be another twenty-five hundred years, when, after Khetchishsht's DNA knit with Koodjuman's corpus callosum, and Satcher Shymee became an Embracer of the Unknown, exposing Koodjuman to the light of the precursor hidden in shadow, that Shymee's DNA ended its dormancy and the first Wielding occurred."

Seest pauses with a headshake, then looks at me. "What no one anticipated was that no two identical Peepl DNA sequences could exist in an active state. Shymee's dormant DNA couldn't come out of dormancy until that Satcher embraced the unknown."

My head cocks back, arms bending at the elbows, palms facing up. "I don't understand. Why wouldn't Shymee and Ibuton have told you that. Certainly, they must have known."

"No. It was a result of their rematerializing. A lot of what is normally known and felt by one of the Peepl was lost with those two, not the least of which were their domains of impelment," Seesterfekt says, smiling. "And without the ability to vanish—also a side effect of rematerializing—they had more than one close call with human hunters and other predators. If ever there were a pair that could have used wings," Seest says, breaking into hearty laughter, "it was those two!"

"So, Koodjuman and I are related by Peepl DNA that was shared from PeePeet through Ketch and Tsits, respectively. But Kirū's line ended with Sivésta and Olūchka, so we're related to her only through the Peepl DNA she preserved and passed on, correct?"

"It's correct that you've been gifted through Koodj Tsitsyoos who passed on her own active, and Ibuton's dormant DNA to you—which of course ended its dormancy as Ibuton embraced the unknown and you received The Wielding. But it's also true that you and Koodjuman both carry a DNA connection to Kirū. You see, my friend, Kirū also had a twin. Her name was Ōnon, and her line remains unbroken through seventy-five thousand years of history. You and Koodjuman are her last two direct descendants. Whether or not Ōnon's line ends, is up to both of you."

My mind races, as does my heart, with the surprise of discovering a mother after a lifetime of not knowing she existed. Joyful tears well up and threaten to breach my eyelids.

"Wait—What?" My joy pops like a soap bubble out of water. "I thought you said Koodjuman and I were the last two remaining of Kirū's line?"

"What I said," Seesterfekt says, in that familiar you-weren't-listening-closely-enough tone, "was, your ancestors trace back to the ***same mother*** living in western Africa, seventy-five thousand years ago. You are the only two humans left of that line. Your DNA is hers, and ***some from hers mixed with ours*** during an attempt to save a molting pair attacked by two members of a neighboring human clan, killed in a vicious fight. Strands of DNA from the molt found their way into that bloodline ***through wounds received in the fight***, and this DNA passed to twin daughters carried at that time, very early in the pregnancy."

Bent forward at the hip, Seest stares at me—a comic waiting for the audience to catch up to the punchline.

I stare back.

Seest shrugs. "Kirū and Ōnon were sis—"

"Yes! I get it! But why do you have to be so god damned cryptic?! Why not just tell it like it is!"

"I did. You asked me the name of the woman injured in the fight trying to defend the molting pair, not the name of your ancestral mother."

My jaw drops.

Seest points.

"Don't!" *You're not getting away that easy...* "You lied about Ibuton's age and you lied about Ibuton's name, didn't you?"

"No, I didn't."

"Yes, you did!"

"Yes, I did." Seest smiles. "You see, sometimes you *do* listen well. Satcher Ibuton's full name was, Ibuton-nin-Tquitnee Peepmot Eezwansa Khamesh-tinikitoopoot Ozo-preejee Tsi-nits-Itchwachoo-kvitsikist."

"Ibuton was the poor bulb that couldn't discern between four different animal's sounds?"

"Yes, well, it was another reason to keep it simple."

"So what did you mean by: *Whether or not Ōnon's line ends, is up to both of you*."

"It's obvious. You're the last two of that line—the last two who can preserve it."

My eyes widen as I fling my arms in front of me with enough force to stop a train. "Whoa-whoa-whoa!"

Seesterfekt is now rolling on the ground, laughing. "Your face!" squeaks a breath between guffaws. "Your face!"

"Did you tell *her* your great idea?" I say, holding my pose. "She'll kill you *and* me!"

Seesterfekt writhes on the ground in hysterics, grasping abdomen, gasping for air.

Am I misunderstanding?...

The writhing stops. "Gender-indoctrinated reasoning." Seest smiles, standing and brushing off. "So predictable."

Embarrassed, I wait, watching Seest stare off.

Human faces... women... children... men.... happy faces... so many different faces... familiarity... kinship... connection... a lifetime of relations with humans... I remember them all, but never met any.

"I let you see that," Seest says.

"I know, thank you."

The frogs continue their planning. One objects to the springtime emerging agreement. They start over, amending their negotiations toward a compromise.

"If you and Koodjuman share your DNA with PeePeet, you'll continue Ōnon's bloodline and reunite Kirū's."

"So you're not suggesting that Koodjuman and I—"

"No, of course not. Your ages are incompatible."

Look whose saying I'm too old...

"Besides, you're right about one thing: She'd kill us both," Seesterfekt says, smiling. "Anyway, what I'm suggesting will guarantee that all three lines continue."

"Wait-wait! Share our DNA with PeePeet? How will that... And what do you mean by all three lines?"

"Yes, if you and Koodjuman share your DNA with PeePeet, she'll molt again and produce a bulb," Seest says, vanishing.

"This has been your purpose from the beginning! Hasn't it?"

Seesterfekt is silent.

"It's the reason you broke from The Forbidden!"

Seest is still silent.

"You saw it coming! Your survival now depends on our survival."

"And perhaps yours depends on ours. Who knows my friend?" Seesterfekt's voice fades in the distance... "Everything changes."

About the Author

A full-time Vermont resident since 1983, J. E. Diaz has worked in the Landscape trade and the Ski industry, and has wandered woods east and west, as well as abroad. In 2016, he began writing and publishing books that reflect his view of the natural world.

His first book, *Wandering Spring, Notes from the Woods of Winhall, Vermont,* is an intimate journey of short stories that introduce his unique perspective.

Following in the footsteps of *Wandering Spring,* his second book, *Wisdom of the Vernal Woods,* weaves nonfiction and fiction against the backdrop of spring woods in Vermont that entertains, inspires, and expands our view of the forest.

In his third book, *The Wielding*, the author weaves non-fiction and fiction, with nature-inspired fantasy–past and present–that takes us to the threshold of an alternate future.

J. E. Diaz lives and writes in Vermont's Green Mountain National Forest.

Your comments are welcome.

jediaz.com

jed@jediaz.com

www.ingramcontent.com/pod-product-compliance
Lightning Source LLC
Chambersburg PA
CBHW030236030426
42336CB00009B/130
9781605715346